The A to Z of ASDs

by the same author

Aspergirls
Empowering Females with Asperger Syndrome
ISBN 978 1 84905 826 1
eISBN 978 0 85700 289 1

**22 Things a Woman Must Know If She Loves
a Man with Asperger's Syndrome**
ISBN 978 1 84905 803 2
eISBN 978 1 84642 945 3

**22 Things a Woman with Asperger's
Syndrome Wants Her Partner to Know**
Illustrated by Emma Rios
ISBN 978 1 84905 883 4
eISBN 978 0 85700 586 1

The A to Z of ASDs

of ASDs

Aunt Aspie's Guide to Life

Rudy Simone

Foreword by Stephen M. Shore

Jessica Kingsley *Publishers*
London and Philadelphia

First published in 2016
by Jessica Kingsley Publishers
73 Collier Street
London N1 9BE, UK
and
400 Market Street, Suite 400
Philadelphia, PA 19106, USA

www.jkp.com

Library of Congress Cataloging in Publication Data
Names: Simone, Rudy, author.
Title: The A to Z of ASDs : Aunt Aspie's guide to life / Rudy Simone ;
  foreword by Stephen M. Shore.
Description: Philadelphia : Jessica Kingsley Publishers, [2016] | Includes
  bibliographical references.
Identifiers: LCCN 2016012061 | ISBN 9781785921131 (alk. paper)
Subjects: LCSH: Asperger's syndrome--Patients--Life skills guides. | Autistic
  children--Life skills guides. | Autistic people--Counseling of.
Classification: LCC RC553.A88 S5674 2016 | DDC 616.85/8832--dc23
LC record available at https://urldefense.proofpoint.com/v2/url?u=https-
3A__lccn.loc.gov_2016012061&d=BQIFAg&c=euGZstcaTDllvimEN8b
7jXrwqOf-v5A_CdpgnVfiiMM&r=4EemtO9R1x-uacXap7EaQ1RHPq9-
MnYBwnfuC-ulpHU&m=g0y7uFJopbrlsDIkA4KNI64PeNFBjIKzBfn16vI
rQ-w&s=TuBtAMzrz9gkQ3LJ8dB4gv7JD2sPXB0nCSBUVGfVlyQ&e=

British Library Cataloguing in Publication Data
A CIP catalogue record for this book is available from the British Library

ISBN 978 1 78592 113 1
eISBN 978 1 78450 377 2

Printed and bound in the United States

Contents

Foreword

Dear Aunt Aspie,

Please tell me what to call your amazing guide to life with Autism Spectrum *Differences* that seems like a dictionary? Or is it a dictionary that's a guide? Once again, Rudy Simone gifts the autism community with straightforward, deeply insightful, and oft controversial, wit garnered from wide-ranging interviews, research and a lifetime as a person on the autism spectrum.

Blasting away myths of autism, such as the lack of desire or need for contact with others, Rudy illuminates terminology, concepts and ideas with the brilliant sunshine of understanding and complete acceptance for who people on the autism spectrum are. For example, the first word *abnormal* is described for what it is, peeling away the negativity that so often accompanies it. Heck…why would someone want to be *normal* after reading her definition?

Literally, from cradle to grave, Ms. Simone expertly explains the person on the autism spectrum in life-affirming guidance ranging from babies and parenting to dealing with depression, anxiety and black and white thinking. Other pearls of wisdom include successful navigation of transition into the adult worlds of effective self-advocacy, employment, relationships of all kinds, employment and other aspects of living amongst the land of grown-ups.

Chock-full of Aspie wisdom, the expertise brought forward in *The A to Z of ASDs* provides ready access to vital techniques and insights that, when employed as needed, empower individuals with autism and those who care for them with powerful strategies for leading fulfilling and productive lives with authenticity.

Most profoundly, *Aunt Aspie* gives us permission and, even more importantly, encouragement to be the unique and different people we are while remaining realistic of the many significant challenges that come with being on the autism spectrum. This *guide*—or is it a *dictionary?*—is a must-read for anyone desiring to gain deeper understanding of what it is like to be autistic, and ultimately what it means to be human.

Stephen M. Shore, Ed.D.
Clinical Assistant Professor at Adelphi University
Internationally known author, speaker and
individual on the autism spectrum

Acknowledgments

To all of my dear friends on and off the spectrum, and my followers on social media. You tolerated my rants and mood swings over the years and were always up for an intelligent chat even when I wasn't.

To my editor, Jessica, for her patience and wisdom.

To Hugo Horiot, for convincing me I still had work, and life, ahead of me.

To my daughter Lena, the one I turn to for comfort, wise counsel and cups of tea.

To Wes, who gives me sage advice and big hugs, no matter where I am in the world.

To Lorraine, who never slammed the door.

To Chris, who gave me love and a much-needed revelation the very day I finished this manuscript.

Thank you all.

Disclaimer

Aunt Aspie is not a psychologist, doctor or nutritionist. All the information in this book is taken from interviews (with autistics and top professionals), life experience, common sense, folk wisdom and research. You are advised to seek the advice of a medical professional if deciding to alter your course of medicine or make any similar changes in diet and lifestyle.

Everyone who reads this book will probably disagree with (or even be offended by) what they read at least once. It is neither our wish nor goal to be politically correct or middle of the road. If that's what you're looking for, you've come to the wrong Auntie's house. There are some mild expletives in this book as well as some candid discussion on sexual matters, matters of violence and other things some people might find upsetting.

Lastly, not everything will apply to all people. And while we have tried to be as comprehensive and thorough as possible, if there are entries or viewpoints we have left out or not devoted as much time to as you'd like, we do apologize. We had to leave books for you to write.

Aunt Aspie is a character of *The Aspergirl Show*™ and is the intellectual property of Rudy Simone. All rights reserved.

Introduction

I'm very fortunate that through writing and music I can communicate my thoughts and feelings to others and usually be understood. However, like many of my readers, off stage and off page, I don't seem to receive the same understanding in daily life. This is the constant dichotomy of Asperger's: the hidden talents, the unspoken insights, the deep waters obscured by a turbulent, troubled or even blank surface. When we are around others and in new or chaotic environments, we process in such a way that while we are focusing on one thing, we may miss others. Whether it is manners, humor, discretion, gracefulness or problem-solving that gets put on hold, it is often difficult for us to show our whole true selves, to be, and give the appearance of, feeling comfortable in our skin, sharp as a tack, or light on our feet, though we may be all of those things at different times.

When I started this book more than three years ago, I wrote, "It is only when I'm alone that I feel like me. It is only when I'm home, looking at the sky, the trees, the lake, the birds, listening to my favorite music, that I feel comfortable and relaxed. Yet, like all humans, I have a need to connect. And like most Aspies, I have a desire to make a difference, to improve the world somehow." Now, I can honestly say that I have learned to love the company of others and, usually, to maintain my sense of self and worth in their presence. This book and the experiences in it have birthed me from my house and put me back on my feet and into the wider world. Even the most autistic person needs others to survive and will form emotional attachments.

Humans are endlessly alluring, fascinating, puzzling, frustrating…and they're everywhere. This is a handbook for the human race, to give you a way in or out of almost any situation, often delivered with a punchline or soundbite to help you remember. Keep it close and call on it when you feel stuck for words, or all alone in the world. Aunt Aspie will always be there with her reassuring presence. She's been there for me since I invented her, and I find her growing into someone I frequently rely on. Kind of like the character of Mrs. Doubtfire, she is a creation I needed to tap into parts of myself that lay dormant. Hers is the voice of reason, experience, wit and wisdom.

Some people are not readers, or think that self-help books are full of theories, interesting but fairly useless facts, and platitudes. This may be a book of words, but it's all about action, putting ideas into practice. I have little patience for things that sound great but are of no real use. I have test-driven most if not all of these ideas and tips, and they work. I got into quite a few accidents and scuffles, ate copious amounts of humble pie, lost and gained face, friends, enemies and more. I'm sure I've a few more of all of those things ahead of me yet. But I find myself making fewer and less drastic mistakes than I used to. One should not be afraid to fall or fail, but you wouldn't go into battle without a sword, shield and commanding officer providing direction, or at least a fellow soldier to watch your back. Here you go.

A

▶ **Abnormal** (see *Normal*) In medical terminology, this would indicate an anomaly that might need attention. For example, an abnormal pain or heart rate. But when it comes to personality and behavior, "abnormal" is really only relative to the majority. By no means should it be immediately equated with "problem." You may simply be eccentric and act in unexpected ways.

You may be abnormally good at something, or have abnormally good senses—many of us do. Abnormal is by no means an inherently derogatory word. The opposite of abnormal is normal, which is a synonym for ordinary…who wants to strive for ordinary?

▶ **Accomplishments** We all have lists of things that we want to accomplish and acquire in our lives: fame, fortune, great career, beautiful partner, etc. Some of us will achieve these things and some will have a harder time. But like a "to-do" list that hangs in your kitchen reminding you that the gutters need fixing and the porch painting, your list will grow and evolve over time. Ours is a never-ending quest for fulfillment.

Accomplishments do play a role in self-esteem. Celebrate each of yours with some ritual of mental gratitude. Set realistic goals, and some less realistic ones. Make efforts to achieve them and accept that virtually every person in this world will leave it with a few items left unticked on the kitchen wall. Feel proud of what you have accomplished, but know that there are other things that give equal pleasure, such as giving, helping, being kind.

For people on the spectrum, you no doubt have a long list. Social issues are usually what stand in the way of achieving our dreams. Read on and learn how to manage these.

▶ **Acting** (see *Gender issues*, *Identity*) We're all actors on this stage. Many of us will fake it till we make it, mimic, mime and memorize our way through life. At some point, this little thing called authenticity will begin to reveal itself to you and let you know what your true character is. You will no longer feel like you must behave a certain way all the time. But acting is necessary. Everyone in the supermarket checkout who says, "Thanks, have a nice day" is acting to a degree, but only the introspective ones realize it. One word of caution: when it comes to friends and relationships, spending your whole life acting means that it will be difficult for others to get close to you and vice versa. Acting may become second nature, to your detriment. Finding your authenticity may take time, but because of all the acting you have done, it's going to be one interesting character that emerges…if you let it.

▶ **ADHD (attention deficit hyperactivity disorder)** I believe, like a lot of honest professionals believe, that ADHD is a myth. That's not to say that you or your child are not jumpy, fidgety, have a hard time concentrating and all the rest; it's just to say that there are a myriad possible causes for that and to lump everyone under this heading doesn't do anyone a service. It makes it easy for the doctor—she can give you a pill. This makes it easier for the teacher—they'll have a more dutiful child in class. It makes it easier for the parent—Johnny can go to his room and do his homework without drama and arguments. And it's wonderful for the pharmaceutical companies—they rack up another 100 billion dollars in profit for the year. Yes, you can take a pill to aid concentration, which I understand can be very helpful for some people, but not others, and as usual there are risks as with all medicines. But, is that how you want to live? Would you not rather figure out the cause? Is it your diet? Chemicals and sugar can wreak havoc. I used to let my little girl have Skittles until I saw her practically levitate, they made her so hyper. Is it food allergies? Lack of exercise? Fluorescent lights? Itchy clothing or other sensory sensitivities? Too much loud TV and commercials every five minutes that interrupt a program and make us forget what we were watching? Is it lack of education? Never having books read to you as a small child, you might not take to them very easily yourself.

When Auntie was a girl, some kids were hyper. They were usually the athletic type, not book lovers. They lived to get out of the classroom and go run and jump and bat balls around or whatever. Others just wanted to hang out in packs, listen to music and flirt. Does your kid (or you) get a chance to do that? Or do you sit and watch TV all day, getting depressed, repressed, suppressed and stressed? All I'm saying is don't believe that every new disorder you hear about is real.

We are not cookie cutter people. The best cure for restless leg syndrome is not a pill, it's Irish river dancing. Maybe the best cure for ADHD is to find something that does actually interest you, instead of trying to make a poet out of a pirate, a mathematician out of a beautician, an exemplary student out of an explorer.

As with all these things, if you are on medication and it is working for you, I'm not saying you should stop taking it. But medication should be the last port of call, especially where children are concerned. I'm also hearing that, like Asperger's, ADHD might be one of those labels doctors are handing out in lieu of more serious things; for example, that there might be a physical cause, or that the child or adult might be very troubled and heading for danger. To define is to limit—to call someone ADHD or Asperger when they are experiencing serious psychological/emotional/mental/spiritual issues, again, does no one any favors. What is the root cause of the problem, if it is a problem?

▶ **Adversity** Life can be a series of lessons and tests. The higher your goals and the loftier your ambitions, the more likely you'll be hitting some roadblocks. Alternatively, if you're heading down the wrong path, you may also stumble into some dark places and dead ends. If you're experiencing a lot of adversity, ask yourself which is the case: are you on the wrong path, or is the universe testing you to see what you're made of? You'll have to figure out which it is. When you are thwarted in some effort, look for the message you're being called to hear or the door that you're being called to open.

Adversity is sometimes called bad luck. Bad luck may be bad karma, the whole "live by the sword, die by the sword" scenario. But I prefer to think of it as this: sometimes things happen as a way of showing us another path. An athlete who is injured may become an artist, an artist who goes blind may become a musician, and so on. You must use every incident to your advantage, even if it means a whole new game.

▶ **Advice** (see *Know-it-all*, *Pedantry*) Getting unsolicited advice is like finding an unwanted caller at your door; it's intrusive, annoying, seeks to sell or convert, and is very likely to be rejected.

Giving unsolicited advice is usually a waste of everyone's time. However, if you feel you must, at least be subtle: "Did you know that such and such is recommended?" "I hear that _____ works really well in some cases." This shows respect for the intelligence and autonomy of the receiver. The direct approach, fraught with words like "you should," "you can't," etc. makes the giver seem controlling and bossy and tends to slam doors rather than open them.

If you have asked for advice, be open to listening. This may sound like a no-brainer, but how many times have we asked and then argued with the giver about why something will not work, without even giving it a minute's consideration?

▶ **Ageism** is the silliest *ism* there is. We're all getting older every day. The only other option is early death. While the body begins to fail and break down at least a little bit, the soul gets more interesting and, barring illness, the mind rich with memory and experience. If you believe in souls, we are all ageless; if you believe the scientific claims that someday we'll all be living to three hundred, then you must realize we are all still children. (See *Bigotry*.)

At the end of the day, the main difference between me and a 24-year-old is that when they sneeze they grab a tissue; I grab…something else.

▶ **Aging on the spectrum** As you get older, you may find that your autistic traits are more prevalent, that you have a lower tolerance for acting normal, like you want to take off your mental girdle and just let it all hang out! Alternatively, some of us feel less autistic as we get older, for various reasons; e.g. acquired knowledge and skills, or in some cases an autism-friendly diet.

In either case, what's beautiful about getting older and is rarely talked about, is finding yourself—the person you were truly meant to be—and no longer trying to conform to society's expectations. That gets exhausting. Personally, the amount of time and energy I wasted trying to be something I could never be, while not nurturing that which I was, is heartbreaking. I can't think of another word for it.

Getting older frees you from those kinds of restrictions. Knowing who you are and acting authentically is real maturity. While we tend to have more responsibilities as we get older—houses, cars, children, grandchildren—we realize that our time is precious and if we want to accomplish our dreams, now is the time. This can make us incredibly productive, creative and just plain fun. Alternatively, we may realize that we've accomplished all we will and we can relax and have more peace in our hearts…less anxiety. These are the gifts of aging.

Incidentally, "act your age" is a command usually uttered by the staid, timid and jealous.

▶ **Androgyny** (see *Gender issues*)

▶ **Anger** is an energy. There are constructive ways to channel it, such as writing a book, taking up jogging or kung fu, starting a movement, writing music and forming a band, making a documentary, starting a petition, going into politics or law. There are destructive ways, such as throwing a chair through a window. You have the power to choose. This book is full of ways to channel anger—righteous or otherwise—and avert destructive meltdowns.

▶ **Animals** I once was watching a detective show in which a grown woman kept mice and this meant, apparently, that she was mentally ill. My hamster and I were seriously offended by that.

We love our animals for so many reasons. Animals are non-judgmental, have simple needs, love us unconditionally, whether we're cool or not, won't steal our lunch money (although I've often thought my dog Tooky would sell me up the river for a cheeseburger) and also they need us, and it's nice to be needed. Part of their appeal may be that we sometimes can control them, train them, make them do what we want. Some of us have fish or cats so this theory admittedly has holes in it, unless there are people out there trying desperately to get Twinkles to swim through a hoop and Felix to roll over. We don't have to make small talk with animals. Communication is largely unspoken and silently understood. We also love them for their aesthetic beauty; I have a cardinal in my back yard who is the bird equivalent of Brad Pitt. They fulfill sensory needs—cuddling, touching, stroking and hugging. (They do also offend some sensory issues.)

Do we humanize animals too much? Perhaps, but I think anyone who's ever had a pet or studied wildlife knows that animals are very emotional creatures. I think that by necessity people have *de*-personified, if that's the right word, animals, to make it okay for us to kill and eat them. So many of us are vegetarians and have a mini- (or not so mini) menagerie at home. Perhaps we identify with their suffering and want to give comfort to as many as we can. Just make sure you can afford it and have enough skills and resources before turning your home into Noah's ark.

▶ **Anti-social** There is a lot of emphasis in most societies on being social. In fact, anyone who is not particularly social may find themselves called *anti-social* as if anyone who doesn't eat ice cream is anti-ice cream. How this reclusiveness is viewed by society changes with time, location and gender—are you a lone wolf or a cat lady? I think it's safe to say most cultures value team players and tribal mentalities and lately this has been taken too far. For the life of me I don't understand why there isn't a diagnosis for people who are pathologically social—who can't spend two days in their own company without falling into a quivering heap, or who need the constant inane banter of daytime talk shows to plug up any random thought that might creep in.

Most truly creative people are quiet and need to spend a lot of time alone with their thoughts, and this doesn't matter if you're a painter, musician, scientist or planner; creativity needs to gestate.

Having said all this, we do need to connect with others or we can get a bit self-centered, if not downright mad. If you find your most frequent conversations are with the spiders on your ceiling and you are frequently busted talking to yourself in grocery store aisles, it's time to break out the proverbial Rolodex (remember those?) and call some friends.

Things you can say if accused of being anti-social:

- "I am not anti-social…I'm *a*social."

- "…I am a social minimalist."

- "…I'm pro-solitude."

▶ **Anxiety** (see *Stress*) I heard Temple Grandin say that anxiety is the primary emotion in Asperger's and that explained and summed up my whole life in an instant. Just like depression isn't the same thing as sadness, anxiety is not the same thing as a legitimate worry. For example, yes, it is worrying if you are short of money, but if you spend every waking moment worrying about everything to the point where it saps your enjoyment of life, that is anxiety.

When an anxiety-prone person arises in the morning, they have to make a conscious effort not to let anxiety rule the day. Remember, we're not looking at life through rose-colored glasses or even clear ones. Our lenses are smeared with the mud of anxiety. Try and remember that and to wash them clear if you can before looking at the world. One way to do this is to think back on all the times you worried about something, only to see it never come to pass. Think of all the wasted hours that could have been spent enjoying something you like. Instead of letting anxiety take hold, cast yourself wholeheartedly into something engrossing, if not enjoyable, to focus your mind more constructively. Action is the enemy of anxiety.

Before joining the hordes of people who follow the pied pipes of Big Pharma, look into diet, exercise and meditation for alleviating anxiety in a healthy, long-term way.

▶ **Approval** You can spend your whole life, in the classroom, the boardroom, the bedroom, looking for approval, the precursor to validation. If you don't approve of you, it doesn't matter who else does. If you do, it almost doesn't matter who else doesn't.

▶ **Arranging things** (see *OCD*) I recently saw a TV show where a forensic psychologist implied that a man was a psychopathic killer by asking him if he arranged his socks by color in a drawer. Aunt Aspie was shocked and appalled! If arranging things were a symptom of mental dysfunction, imagine how difficult buying groceries in a supermarket would be... "Excuse me, can you tell me where the pasta is?" "I don't know lady, your guess is as good as mine... somewhere." Neatness and tidiness means there is one less thing to confuse us in our day.

Some of us take it to an extreme level. Those people make good overseers, organizers, engineers, teachers, administrators, all sorts of things. But, if there's something you're fanatical about, like keeping the DVDs in alphabetical order, mix them up for a while, because no matter how you like to keep things in their place, sometimes life steps in and steals your crayon.

Aunt Aspie says: "I don't have control issues. I do, however, have a problem with chaos."

▶ **Asperger's** When I first heard the term, it sounded like a rude word. Asperger's may *sound* like a hot beef patty sandwich taken from the wrong end of a cow, but it's actually a condition on the autism spectrum.

Advocacy and awareness There's been a lot of bad press about autism spectrum disorders and many of us have been making attempts to counteract it, to debunk the myths. There are ways of being a force for change in the world of Asperger's: directly, e.g. by writing books, running forums or groups, giving or arranging talks and more. There are other ways too, like by being successful at whatever you're doing, while being "out" about your Asperger's syndrome (AS). It would be wonderful if some actor or film director would announce that he or she was on the spectrum while receiving their Oscar, but perhaps you can be the first!

As a label (see *Diagnosis*, *Labels*) The only reason Asperger's was left out of the fifth edition of the *Diagnostic and Statistical Manual of Mental Disorders* (DSM-5) is that no one could agree on the correct way to pronounce it. I'm kidding of course, but labels are often arbitrary and certainly change with the times. Labels are explanations, ways to group people. What benefit do the labels *autistic* or *Aspie* provide? They give you a frame of reference to explain your qualities and experiences. They give you a community to talk to and learn from, inspire and be inspired by. They also give you a body of work to read, view or listen to.

In order for various factions and subcultures to integrate and celebrate what we have in common, there first has to be acknowledgement of what we don't have in common. It's part of the process of growth of society and the human race. But it wouldn't be necessary if there weren't some pain and some inequalities that need to be redressed.

For school-age children/young adults there may also be benefits in education protocols, and in some cases there may be employment protection or assistance.

As an obsession It's nice to get together with your tribe and talk about the thing that binds you and we tend to do that a lot when we first discover Asperger's. It's like any minority, whether sexual, ethnic, neurological, etc. We can be militant by necessity, at first. But there's more to life, and other things to have in common with other people. People who can only talk about this one thing have turned self-discovery and pride into an unhealthy obsession. It could almost be wondered if they don't really want things to get better because then they won't have a cause anymore. To define oneself as a minority may very well be necessary for a while, but then it must become about empowerment, not pity; strengths in action. If that's all you talk about, perhaps it's time to widen your horizons; it's a thin line between pride and prejudice.

In the media Some people want to make their mark on the world and exert their influence, and if they cannot do it in a positive way, and if they are desperate, or mentally ill, they will do so any way they can. Many of us, particularly school-age children, have had a direct negative experience because of media stupidity blaming recent mass shootings on Aspies. You can try to avoid this topic, but even if you don't have network TV, you really couldn't avoid it unless you lived on a deserted island. Many of my friends told me their kids were upset by the reports in the news saying a killer had Asperger's or was on the autism spectrum. There was a ripple effect in schools, offices and communities, of events and behaviors being blamed erroneously on Asperger's. News anchors were "diagnosing" killers as being "somewhere on the spectrum."

The fact is, an Aspie is much more likely to be the victim of violent crime than the perpetrator. It is far more likely that these disturbed individuals were mentally ill with conditions that share traits with Asperger's. It is also possible, if not likely, that sometimes people are misdiagnosed unintentionally or even intentionally—it would be far easier to tell a parent their child had AS instead of some psychopathology. Many conditions have overlapping traits, but I've come up with a simple way to explain the difference between a kid with Asperger's and one with other psychological conditions that sometimes get mistaken for AS. Yes, it's a generalization but it does a good job in a soundbite: *Aspies want to make the world a better place, sociopaths don't care about it, psychopaths want to tear it down.*

▶ **Authenticity** is about acting on your true feelings and beliefs, knowing who you are. It is fluid, ever-changing, always challenged. It is the ongoing process of self-discovery and sharing that true self with others. It may be difficult for us on the spectrum to have this sense and knowledge of self at first. We may feel like impostors or aliens at times, especially when young, or we may have been ridiculed or bullied for our differences and learned to hide our true selves. We become actors. But acting is a mask, and every mask gets stifling after a time. At some point we must take that risk and take off the mask. It gets easier: as experience and nurture add to genetics and fill us up, we become fully fleshed-out persons. There will be those who embrace you.

▶ **Autism, causes of** No one knows for certain what causes autism but the general and scientific consensus is that it is a combination of genetics (it runs in families) and environmental factors. No one gene has been pinpointed; it may more likely be gene interactions or mutations. Similarly, no specific environmental factors have been identified, only suspected.

The following is from my website Help for Aspergers[1] and is based on research and discussion with some of the world's top scientists and researchers in the field.

> Autism is a developmental disorder. Because brain development follows a complicated series of delicately timed events beginning early in gestation and continuing through infancy and into early childhood, environmental insults may occur at numerous time-points, each with a distinct imprint in terms of the processes affected and the intensity of the impact—what those environmental factors are has not been determined with any certainty.

> There is also strong evidence to support the theory that autism begins in the digestive system, which has been compromised by genetics and, further, by poor diet

and environmental factors; it is essentially a "leaky gut." Some say autism can be cured or at least diminished by following a strict diet, such as the GFCF (gluten-free, casein-free) diet. It is thought that when gluten and casein (found in grains such as wheat and most dairy products) are broken down into peptides, they may pass through imperfections in the intestines. These peptides act like morphine in the body and can adversely impact brain development.

A digestive system which does not contain healthy ora (good bacteria) cannot eliminate toxins, and allows bad things to pass into our bloodstream. It also cannot get the most nourishment from our food. According to authors Donna Gates and Dr. Natasha Campbell-McBride, who separately came to the same conclusion, the modern western diet, which has spread around the world, is essentially the root cause of the worldwide spread of autism. While the idea of a "cure" for autism may be increasingly unpopular in the spectrum community, these two researchers postulate that one just has to eat the correct food to dramatically lessen autistic traits: a mostly plant-based diet with an emphasis on fermented foods. Watch a short six-part video presented by Gates and Campbell-McBride on YouTube.[2]

I heard a science news report a few years ago about some bacteria that's only found in the intestines of autistic people which might lead to an autism "blood test" but so far that is not, to my knowledge, forthcoming.

Observing children's brainwaves may also allow identification of autism earlier than is currently possible, and can judge severity of autism, as discussed in an article from HealthDay,[3] but it does not address causes of autism.

▶ **Autism spectrum disorders (ASDs)** This is the current terminology in the DSM-5[4] and other diagnostic manuals. I prefer the term *autism spectrum conditions*, but unfortunately it never really caught on. Asperger's was subsumed into this category. Without splitting hairs over terminology, the current accepted criteria describe deficits in social communication and interaction that persist over time and throughout a variety of situations. Also, repetitive behaviors, activities, actions and interests that seem restricted if not restrictive. These traits and others must appear in the first two or three years of life and they must cause "clinically" significant impairment of functions across most areas of life, such as work and relationships with others.

This is not a book that is going to engage in debates over terminology and criteria. Auntie is well aware that most of us, especially girls, did not have our autistic traits recognized early enough to qualify under this, or that they didn't impact us significantly until puberty. We're also aware that often Asperger's is listed as an autism disorder, but in other places, as a related disorder. It is the attempt of five blind men, each clutching a different part of the animal, to describe an elephant.

What this book will do instead is provide information that is useful to anyone who falls anywhere on the spectrum, from the rather useless PDD-NOS (pervasive developmental disorder not otherwise specified) moniker, to Asperger's, to our cousins the narcissists and egocentrics, even if they only have one toe on the ribbon of autism.

▶ **Awkward** (see *Normal*) For a long time, I felt that calling certain AS behaviors awkward was reminiscent of the European view of non-whites in the age of exploration, wanting to "tame the savages," instead of appreciating differences and altering their own behavior and mindset.

However, there is absolute truth in majority rules. If you bring one non-autistic into a room with spectrum folks, guess who's the awkward one? Given the customs of the day, there are certain things that people do that draw unwanted attention to themselves, and they may be things that can be addressed and changed. Autistic folks process differently, and may be tuning in to a whole bunch of different frequencies than non-autistics in any given situation. To borrow the overused alien analogy, this planet is loud and busy and full of things that seem pretty nonsensical to us. If the most easy-going non-autistic person was thrust into an environment where everything was alien, they'd be awkward as well.

The tricks in this book will include sensory tools, cognitive tools, diet, self-awareness, self-image, social skills practice and more to help minimize how awkward you feel in your daily life and to help you on your way to feeling great in your skin and in many social settings.

B

▶ **Babies** (see *Parenting*)

▶ **Being taken advantage of** In our desire to please and be helpful, we are often malleable, gullible and easy to take advantage of, especially when young. I was only twelve when a neighborhood drug dealer asked me to take a bag of marijuana to the mall to sell. I immediately seized upon the opportunity to have something to say to other kids. I wanted to make friends, and having a purpose, a script, would make it easier. Luckily, or perhaps unluckily, I was never caught.

We with Asperger's learn by mimicking. We mimic those around us, especially non-autistics (NAs). When we mimic someone, we don't challenge them. We go along with what they say and do, learning how to be like them. We can also be fairly expressionless, seem less emotional. All these things mean that other people may think that we'll go along with whatever they want us to do and, like Spock, we'll never lose our cool. That may be true for a while. It can take ages for us to understand that someone does not have our best interest at heart. But once you push us too far, we realize we can't trust you, and that you have betrayed our trust, we may have a huge meltdown and burn our bridges, cutting you out of our life completely.

If something feels jarring to you—a situation or request— honor your feelings and your gut. If something is illegal, your choice has been made for you: don't do it. Sometimes we get pushed or bullied into things. Turn to whomever you can for help and guidance. It takes time to discern when we're being taken advantage of, and practice to avoid or deflect it. We're not used to advocating for ourselves even if we are adept at doing this for others. But the mind is a growing and flexible organ. You can and will learn to stand up for yourself without having to get to meltdown point.

▶ **Bigotry** happens when people are bored and disgruntled with their own lives, but rather than do something constructive about that, they choose to pick on some minority or subculture instead. Hitler did that, and millions of people jumped on his bandwagon, suddenly blaming Jews for their own lack of jobs or whatever. Cultures around the world and throughout history have blamed women who were a little different, especially if they had red hair or some other "mark of the devil," for being witches, and attributed all sorts of life's problems to them, from a drought season to a sick cow to a rash of plague.

Currently 76 countries have made homosexuality illegal and some state supreme courts are still trying to defy the US Supreme Court's decision which made gay marriage legal in 2015. This confounds me. If you don't believe in gay marriage, you're in luck: no one's going to force you into one anytime soon. Most of these bigots say things like "Gays flaunt it, and I don't want to have to think about gays having sex." I say, "Honey, I don't wanna think about you and your wife having sex either, but you don't see me trying to make you illegal." Whatever happened to "clean up your own backyard," "let he who has not sinned cast the first stone," and all those other bits of basic folk wisdom? I personally think that those who hate the most are in envy to a large degree.

Where we Aspies are concerned we've each experienced prejudice and bullying on a personal level. Could you imagine if it was illegal to give birth to a child on the spectrum, or if we suddenly had to go through intensive therapy to cure us of our aberration? If you are prejudiced against any subculture, you're not thinking it through.

▶ **Black and white thinking** is a hallmark of AS. Most things in life are not black and white. There are more than fifty shades of grey, there are a million. Very rarely is someone completely in the right, or completely in the wrong. Thinking in absolutes is exhausting, and is one of our more unpleasant traits.

One typical Aspie black and white thought is "If I make a mistake I *am* a mistake." Sometimes just pointing that out to yourself whenever it occurs is enough to begin to defeat that defeatist attitude. The key here is learning to accept that *everyone* makes mistakes, even the most successful people, and we never stop making them: it's part of being human. But we learn from them, pick ourselves up, dust ourselves off, and go forward. Once you realize and accept this, it really is the key to mental freedom and even physical freedom in that you won't be so afraid to venture out and try again.

▶ **Bluntness** Being blunt is like giving someone a present without a wrapper, whether they want it or not. The things I try to ask myself before acting like the verbal equivalent of the whomping willow, are, "Am I being mean, or am I being kind? Am I serving myself or someone else?"

We can all become much more mindful of our impact on other people, more tactful. We may be blunt for the following reasons:

- Expediency and honesty. Why waste time, mince words?

- There is a person I think I don't really want in my life, so I say something a bit incendiary to see how they react. Aspies are not huge on collecting acquaintances, so we aren't going to amass large numbers of friends we don't philosophically jive with, the way we see non-autistics do.

- If it happens suddenly, for example at a party, it may be because we feel cornered and need an emergency escape route, and this will certainly blow one open like a grenade thrown at a wall.

The danger of this behavior is that it is destructive, often irreversible, and can get you an unwanted reputation. Tact, the opposite of bluntness, is a fine art form that we can all master or at least get better at.

▶ **Body image** (see *Diet, Eating disorders*) Many of us on the spectrum have no idea what we look or sound like to others. We often have a far worse idea than the reality. Perhaps because so many of us feel "less than" simply because we aren't treated very well, or are bullied, we begin to feel there must be something visibly wrong with us. We can become very withdrawn, inward, small. And now in this computer-driven world, Aspies and non-Aspies alike treat our bodies more like furniture than machines, something to support our "head drive." The one good thing that's come out of that is the practice of taking and uploading profile pictures; many of us heretofore camera-shy Aspies are hamming it up daily, egged on by our bevy of admirers, usually fellow Aspies.

Every day, make sure your to-do list contains a fair bit of exercise. Getting cool clothes and haircuts is all well and good, but most of us Aspies think that people who wear a lot of makeup and have processed hair and fake tans (not to mention boobs) look phony and we hate phony. Work with what you've got in a way that brings out your inner beauty. You've got to hang on to yourself; you'll never be anybody else.

Lastly, some of us take longer to develop at puberty, or never get as buxom as we wish. You know you're flat-chested when you mistake your sleep mask for your bra…and it fits. Remember, if you don't get big, buff and busty early on, there's less to sag later when mean old Mr. Gravity works his number on you like he does with everybody.

Remember, anyone can get a stylist, not everyone can get an intellect.

▶ **Breakups** (see *Rejection, Respect and self-respect*) For some of us, this is the hardest transition you'll ever face besides birth, death and the end of *Harry Potter*. Because we may lack theory of mind—realizing that other people have thoughts and feelings different to our own—we may not understand or comprehend that someone we love passionately does not love us back. While I don't buy into the theory that one-sided love is merely obsession, I do believe that one-sided love is unhealthy and needs to be dealt with accordingly. Loving anyone who doesn't love you back can be debilitating.

In the aftermath of a breakup, you'll have the added difficulty of hormones, and a physical craving that is not going to be satisfied by the person you desire ever again. Truth be told, it's possible you may never meet someone who will make you feel quite as enraptured, but chances are you will.

Some of us will chase our ex for one more fix, one more attempt to seduce them back into our fold. That is a massive waste of time, and it's a very dangerous position to put yourself in emotionally and psychologically, not to mention physically, for you don't know what they've been up to since they left you, and legally, for there's a fine line between obsessor and stalker.

You will probably needs lots of counseling if you are having difficulty wrapping your head around the fact that they are gone, or you may need friends and family to help. Most of us resist this, as we don't want to hear what other people plainly see—that the person who left you doesn't love you. We may lash out, tell everyone they're wrong, cry ourselves to sleep at night wondering where they are, who they are with, what they're doing. And we'll bang our heads against the wall trying to figure out how they can live with themselves, how they can forget us and move on when we can't.

Do whatever brings you comfort and occupies your mind. While I'm not usually in favor of ignoring feelings, if they are too painful and raw to examine clearly, you'd best leave them alone for a while and come back to them in a bit. So keep busy, take up things you've always wanted to, like tap dancing, French or sky diving (with a parachute, obviously), as opposed to something self-harming. It's probably not super-helpful to hate your ex either, although if they were a world-class stinker, buying a blow-up doll that resembles them and punching it around never hurt anyone. (Not that I've ever done that.)

Sometimes it's not so much a case of the person not loving you, it's a case of compatibility. Only time will show you, and it always does, that the person and you were not meant to be, and the reason will be made clear in time. Once Aunt Aspie loved a man who was an investment banker. He now works on Wall Street. Now that I am older and wiser I realize that living in Manhattan is like kryptonite to me—and I don't think my goats and chickens would like it either. I never would have been able to manage it, and I would never have been happy. It doesn't mean I didn't love him, and I probably always will. That is some of the bittersweet poetry of life.

"Crying is all right in its way while it lasts. But you have to stop sooner or later, and then you still have to decide what to do," wrote C.S. Lewis in *The Silver Chair*,[5] and that quote has stayed with me. I think that's why I never stay down for long. After the storm, comes the quiet. We can pretend the thing that made us cry never happened and carry on but I think that's only going to take us back to the same crossroad. It's better to acknowledge that something has happened, even possibly that nothing will ever be the same; so what should we do now? We cannot control the actions of others, make them see our inner beauty and pure intentions, so we must be selfish and ask ourselves, "What do *I* want at this moment? What if the person who hurt me didn't exist? What would I be doing right now?" It might take days, weeks or months to answer, but isn't it better to dream of possibilities than to lament impossibilities?

▶ **Budgeting** (see *Money*)

▶ **Bullying** (see *Being taken advantage of*) It is perhaps easier to abuse people on the spectrum because we are different. We don't seem to react the expected way in many situations, so we are poked at and prodded to see what we're made of like a cruel scientific experiment. Auntie knows the horrors of bullying far too well, and the havoc it can wreak on an otherwise peaceful mind, even when the bullying isn't physical. While a certain amount of adversity is inevitable in life, and necessary for growth, bullying is poison. It can cause illness, depression and even drive someone to violence or suicide.

If you are being bullied, you need to speak up. Find friends, parents, teachers, bosses, someone who will listen, for reasons of offloading and perhaps intervention if needed. Trying to make peace with the bully might work, although I know that won't be an option for some of you. Many of us use humor to make us unthreatening to, if not popular with, bullies. You can try to joke with them, maybe turn it into a relationship of friendly banter, giving as good as you get. While some of us will loathe even the thought of trying to play that way, a lot of Aspies do use comedy to make friends and defuse and deflect potentially hazardous situations. It's a way to take control by making everyone see things in a new way and by making them laugh.

Others take up team sports to create a camaraderie with potential bullies. This can apply to school or work, since some employers have sports teams. Even if yours doesn't, playing a team sport can give you insight into and respect for different personality types. It can also give you more confidence.

Workplace bullying training and awareness is never going to catch on the way perhaps it should. Adults are expected to behave and to handle themselves. Adult bullying is often the insidious type—gossip, ostracizing, isolation— and can be as painful and debilitating as it is for school-age children. Bullies, in school and work, are often more popular with the authorities than the ones they victimize.

Their seeming confidence and control of the boardroom or classroom means one less person for the principal or boss to think about. In reality, they cause countless lost days at work and school, whether directly through fear, or indirectly, through real illnesses caused by fear and stress.

If you're being bullied as an adult, it is probably going to bring up all the shame, guilt and confusion of the child Aspie in you. Every situation will require individual analysis and response. Counseling with someone who knows AS is going to help, as will knowing what your rights are. The Workplace Bullying Institute has some excellent resources and they've been around for a while.[6] (See *Employment and self-employment.*)

Some schools claim to have zero tolerance for bullying. This typically heavy-handed approach will never work. School culture can influence the moral code of students to a degree, but you can't legislate away emotional drama, you can only bring it out of the shadows, listen to it, and try to understand it. Once my daughter was being bullied at school; a girl shoved her against a locker. All the other kids intervened and protected my Lena. But they didn't ostracize and revile the aggressor. They were kind to her and spoke to her sense of reason. It turns out she came from a tumultuous home and was having problems there, and so she was taking her anger and frustration out on someone who seemed to be happy. Showing compassion to everyone from all angles was the magic bullet here, and I'm glad to know there are children in the world with big hearts and this kind of common sense.

Bullying is a buzzword at the moment so there's a danger of it being overused. It's not bullying if someone disagrees with you or pokes a little fun now and then.

Lastly, those bullies who torment you are usually nothing to fear in the long run. A girl who literally drove me out of school decades ago recently had *Kung Fu Panda 3* listed as her favorite film on social media. 'Nuff said.

▶ **Burning bridges** (see *Being taken advantage of*) There was a song my gran used to play in which a man sang "burning bridges behind me." In true little kid form I thought he was singing "burning britches behind me." Ouch. Both can be uncomfortable and get you running fast and far without really thinking about where you are going. Both can get you hurt.

Some of us have burned so many it's like we're trapped on an island, seemingly with no escape, no way out, no way back and no way forward. Until recently I had felt that way and operated that way since my late teens. One or two slights, whether real or imagined, could get you crossed off my guest list forever. That list got slimmer and slimmer until I hardly had any friends left at all. I finally vowed to be more tolerant, patient, forgiving. While I still struggle with not whipping out my proverbial red pen every time someone cheeses me off, I'm getting better. Much better.

Part of my problem was not choosing my friends carefully, and the other part is what Jennifer O'Toole says in her book *Asperkids*: "friendly and friend are fuzzy boundaries."[7] There are so many different levels of friend, acquaintance, relative or colleague and we as Aspies tend to demand the highest and best from each one. No one can live up to our own personal standards, because they have their own. You can't demand the same loyalty, understanding and treatment from everyone. People aren't put on the earth to please you.

But no matter if they are friend, stranger, relative or lover, scratch the surface of every person and you will find flaws. Cast off everyone who makes mistakes, and we will surely be alone. Forgiving others and keeping them in our roster of friends is a very good character-building exercise for all of us.

C

▶ **Candida** (see *Diet*) I've included this because *Candida albicans* is basically an intestinal flora that is necessary and present in everyone, but when there is too much, it begins to break down the mucous lining in the gut wall, leading to leaky gut. Hence there is an autism connection. It is worth knowing this, and reading books specific to candida diets and leaky gut syndrome.

▶ **Character** is defined as the mental and moral qualities distinctive to an individual. When we say someone has character, we usually mean good character, for example doing what is right even when it isn't easy. Character is formed in many ways—how we are raised, educated—but also can be forged in the fires, meaning that those with the hardest knocks can sometimes have the greatest character. There's no recipe. It seems to be genetics, environment and choice. Free will. Choosing to be honest, kind, brave or a number of other traits is, for the most part, in our grasp. I do find that in the broad sense of having good character, Aspies are naturally heroic. It doesn't mean we aren't flawed, but there seems to be a built-in switch that flips off when it sees cruelty, unfairness and other undesirables.

▶ **Clichés** Little children don't use clichés, they speak from their hearts and minds and imaginations, and so communication, if rudimentary, is authentic. It isn't until we get older that bumping fists and high-fiving become an issue. If you dislike clichés, you aren't alone. While we all fall into the lazy trap of using them, words like *awesome*, while catchy, show a deplorable lack of imagination; *hater* is used mainly to silence those who disagree, while *bitch* serves a similar function with a sexist twist. *Keepin' it real* is the corniest, most unreal expression of them all. Auntie's recent peeves are *selfie* and *trending*. Whoever made those last two deserves a walloping with a cliché rubber chicken. While we may fall into the trap like any human, I think many Aspies feel clichés are the language of the non-autistic. Give us Shakespeare or Elvish, things we can sink our mental teeth into. Using clichés now and then is fine, but feel free to speak in full, complete sentences using traditional English and correct grammar. Watch people stare in amazement as they wonder how you know such big words.

By the way, here are some alternatives to awesome: breathtaking, awe-inspiring, magnificent, wonderful, amazing, stunning, staggering, imposing, stirring, smashing (very Austin Powers), impressive, formidable, fearsome, dreaded, mind-boggling, mind-blowing, jaw-dropping, excellent, marvelous, very good, wondrous. (Of some interest, originally, awesome meant *awful*.)

▶ **Clothing** (see *Shopping: Buying clothes*)

▶ **Cognitive issues** (see *Executive function*) According to the Center for Disease Control, "Cognitive impairment is when a person has trouble remembering, learning new things, concentrating, or making decisions that affect their everyday life. Cognitive impairment ranges from mild to severe."[8] The autism spectrum disorders occur at all intelligence levels, but all of us will have unevenly developed cognitive skills. These are too many to list, but are scattered throughout the book as separate entries, such as prosopagnosia.

▶ **Comorbids** Because the autistic brain is wired differently, like a series of highways in which some connect at hyperspeed while others are sluggish and still others are under construction, there are bound to be lots of other subsequent, co-occurring conditions, commonly referred to as comorbids. Here's is a short list, found on Wikipedia: anxiety, attention deficit hyperactivity disorder, bipolar disorder, bowel disease, developmental coordination disorder, epilepsy, fragile X syndrome, intellectual disability, neuroinflammation and immune disorders, nonverbal learning disorder, obsessive compulsive disorder, Tourette syndrome, sensory problems, tuberous sclerosis, sleep disorders, other mental disorders.[9]

Some of these are proven, some are only theoretically connected to autism and not all of them affect everyone on the spectrum. And within those comorbids are yet more subcategories. For example, under developmental coordination disorder you find things like proprioception difficulties and under epilepsy, blackout seizures, which may occur without full-blown epilepsy being present. Yikes!

There are some people on the spectrum who seem to take pleasure in plundering the depths of the DSM and PubMed to find a diagnosis for every trait or symptom that they have. Others are a little more down to earth, preferring to say, "I'm not good with math" over "I have dyscalculia," Or, "I'm not good at sports" rather than "I have dyspraxia." Let's face it, we can turn absolutely anything into a diagnosis, a condition and a comorbid if we choose to.

Personally, the only time I use the word is when I think of Gomez and Morticia. Now there's a couple of comorbids I like. But of course, I don't want to downplay the reality for some of us. With autism spectrum conditions comes a smorgasbord of potential other conditions. How to label and use them is up to you, and if you're seriously affected there are all sorts of ways to overcome or improve these conditions.

My word of caution is to avoid labeling everything about yourself. It's alienating to other people and makes you sound a bit self-obsessed and, further, obsessed with being different or flawed. Thinking you are one giant bundle of isms, ergers, axias and ulias can definitely lead to the disability armchair, where you think you will always be unable to be a functioning, happy human being.

▶ **Competitiveness** Women and men on the spectrum tend not to be very competitive individuals. We strive to reach our inner ideals, or maybe strive to reach the creative heights of our heroes in science, literature and art. We may be shocked to find that there are people in the world who want to compete with and possibly even sabotage us. They may try to steal our ideas, our reputations, our property, even our boyfriends, girlfriends or spouses. Such behavior is alien to most of us. However, to loosely quote one of my favorite stories, those who do not wield swords can still die upon them. In other words, my friends, there comes a time in your life when you have to fight, whether you want to or not.

If there is a job you'd like, a solo you'd be good at, a piece of fruit that you desire, sometimes it's nice to step aside and let others have it, but if you do this your whole life, you will always be a 'might have been' kind of person. Don't be afraid to be proactive sometimes and go after what you want. You deserve it as much as the next person.

As for the unethical type of competitors, you must fight against those poor but insidious souls who do not have an original thought in their puny little heads so they have to try and steal yours. Fight with every inner and sometimes outer (legally of course) resource you have.

▶ **Compliment** (see *Self-esteem*) Being able to take a compliment graciously is one of life's littlest pleasures, and one of our greatest challenges. Best not to overthink whether it is sincere, deserved or some sort of trick. Best just to say, "Thank you."

▶ **Condescension** is a weapon used by the truly insecure. If someone shows you condescension, try not to knee-jerk but have a little compassion for their own insecurity while showing that you are nobody's fool with a polite but firm response, if at all possible. Sometimes a little humor can help; for example, a nurse recently told me to "suck it up" when I winced in pain during an emergency room visit. "Honey," I said, "pain like this won't fit through a straw." It didn't make her less of a jerk but it made me less of a victim.

▶ **Confidence vs. arrogance** Confidence opens doors, socially and professionally. Someone who possesses skills but no confidence might not get their chance to shine. Confidence is conveyed through words and body language. Hunched shoulders, lack of eye contact, mumbled responses: these are door slammers.

A certain amount of confidence helps other people feel relaxed around you, and feel safe in your presence, if not your hands. Picture a pilot getting onto a plane looking downcast, worried, nervous, fidgety. Now picture another with his head held high, a firm gaze and a steady hand. Which plane would you want to travel in? Try to picture yourself as confident not based on any sort of myth or fantasy, but based on what you know, what you do, and what you deserve. Spectrum folks tend to swing between too humble and too cocky. This is not good because it's jarring to other people and makes you seem too extreme. It's better to find a happy medium.

Arrogance is not necessarily confidence taken too far. Scratch the surface of it and you'll probably find insecurity, fear, frustration and pain. It's very scary putting yourself or your work in front of people and so we may overcompensate, trying to force our fears and vulnerabilities away. Strike a balance. One way to avoid this issue is to ask others about themselves and not make yourself the object of conversation or constant thought. It is true that sometimes you have to toot your own horn if no one else will, but don't be a blowhard.

▶ **Conflict and confrontation** I can feel my throat constrict, my heart race, my chest tighten and my mind begin to ache just typing the words. We Aspies are as cut out for conflict and confrontation as fish are to run a five-mile race. In some ways, we can be the peacemakers in the family. Those with classically autistic children know not to raise the voice, argue, get into it when the child is around or the child will let them know in no uncertain terms that they are upsetting them. We at the other end of the spectrum are less tolerated in our hissy fits, so we tend to just bottle up, go to our rooms, slap on headphones and stare at a book or device.

In the lunchroom, if someone tries to steal our tater tots, we're more likely to pretend that nothing's happening than to defy our would-be burger burglars. Until, of course, it's too late, and our lid is essentially flipped (see *Meltdowns*). Learning to self-advocate and ask questions (without being shrill) can reduce the chance that things will get to this point. While I don't think confrontation will ever be enjoyable for us, disagreements happen and it isn't necessarily the end of the world, relationship, etc.

We may also be hyper-vigilant from post-traumatic stress disorder (PTSD) and that Aspie sixth sense, so may learn to avoid confrontation quite skillfully, but sometimes it simply cannot be avoided. Taking care of your nerves with good diet and exercise will strengthen your nervous system and make you less likely to fall apart.

▶ **Consideration for others** One of the problems with social isolation and living inside our own heads is that other people can become sort of abstract. Most Aspies I know are kind to others, but we can often be Scrooge-like in our everyday proclamations. That's why Facebook and other social media, as well as AS groups, are important for building social skills, but they can also be virtual playgrounds, with roaming cyberbullies waiting to pop up on your post and hijack your thread the way they used to steal your lunch money. We need to remember the human element in the equation.

Part of the reason for this is the decline in popularity of kindness. There's an epidemic of reality shows out there that promote and reward cutthroat behavior and have even turned singing into a competitive sport. I don't watch them, but I have heard about the girl who killed herself after being humiliated on national television by one of her idols. People have a funny way of not realizing they're supporting and reinforcing this cutthroat culture. One of the greatest examples of this was the death of Princess Diana. Most of the people crying and shouting that the press killed her were the very people who bought the magazines that paid photographers to hound her relentlessly. This was a lack of consideration for another person taken to its extreme. Basic consideration for others, or lack of it, is at the root of most if not all of society's ills. Having consideration for others will cure most of what ails us.

People literally will climb over one another to get to the top, but like crabs in a barrel, all we do is succeed in pulling all of us down. Consideration for others means we actually have to think of something besides our own wants and needs. "Inconsideration" is not a malicious intent, it's an absence of caring. In real life, I find Aspies to be some of the most considerate people there are. Just watch those i-muscles.

▶ **Conversation** is not a game of solitaire. It's more like a slow game of practice tennis, but with the aim of keeping the ball in play rather than beating the other person. We on the spectrum do have a tendency to monologue and not notice that others are growing impatient. If others are bored with a topic of conversation they will look away, say nothing, try to change the subject, or try to get away. Stop every few sentences to see if others are engaged in the discussion. If someone appears bored, talking longer and louder is not going to make it appealing for them.

Aspies generally like to talk about ideas and things like films or TV shows, as well as what their special passions are. Non-autistics do this very same thing, quite a bit, but they also talk about their friends more than we do. They tend to use words like *she* and *he* a lot in their conversations. They talk with friends about friends and what they're up to.

If you're bored with a conversation, try not to roll your eyes, or say something blunt or rude. Even if it's shallow and you really can't swim in the puddle, just smile and nod politely and in your head, contemplate something interesting, like formulas, your next invention, or space travel.

▶ **Counseling** I recommended to a friend on the spectrum they seek counseling for what seems like a lifelong habit of being negative and morose. They negatively and morosely replied that it probably wouldn't help. The hardest part of counseling is getting started. Finding someone who truly understands AS issues is a must. There are a few listed on my website, Help for Aspergers.[10] They also need to be someone you feel comfortable talking to, at least within reason.

During years of misdiagnosis many of us got poor advice, bad judgments and wrong referrals/treatment as a result. Things have moved on. If you are struggling, spinning your wheels, and feel you need a kick starter to move forward, talking to a person with a certain amount of emotional distance and perspective can be enormously helpful. Some issues are minor, transient and can be addressed easily; others are much more lifelong and deep-seated, and can take months or years with a good counselor to fix. Happiness is our birthright and if you have not been able to find yours, this might be a good place to start.

▶ **Creativity** (see *Savant, Eidetic and photographic memory*) Art is often seen as a luxury, the artist as a child who refuses to grow up. Is a song less important than a house? A story less important than a factory? Build one of the latter, people will think your work substantial. Yet look at this world and ask where we all would be without music, paintings, stories, sculptures, films, etc.

From painting to code-writing, engineering to composing, most people on the spectrum are engaged in some sort of creative activity whether as a hobby or a job. Even classically autistic people can be talented pianists and painters. The "lack of social imagination" criteria seemed to have lodged in the collective brain, and morphed into "lack of imagination" full stop, and the education/job trajectory visualized by and for young adults on the spectrum was planned around and limited by this kind of thinking.

If you have a child on the spectrum, you will have seen for yourself how diligent they are at whatever pursuits they are engaged in, and if it's a creative pursuit, how prolific they can be. I think that perhaps we attract more naysayers than non-autistics because we don't have the confidence and the savvy and the cool we associate with artistic types. This was evidenced by the audience and judges' reaction to Aspergirl Susan Boyle's debut performance, their unspoken thought: "How could such an uncool person sing so well?"

Artists are often accused of being self-obsessed, but perhaps it is more about creating something that will last, enrich, provoke, entertain, enlighten, compel, sadden, delight and make possible the thought of the divine. No one accuses the football player of being obsessed with self, partly because he plays with teammates. Other athletes work without teammates but you still don't hear the same standard of measure applied. Both the artist and the athlete do what they do for the same reasons—because they're good at it, because they're compelled, and for the public, for anyone who might appreciate the artistry, the message, the effort put into it.

Creativity saves lives daily—those who are alone can bemoan their state and the silence, or they can flex creative muscles and fill their hours with art: gems that will eventually reach out like a beacon to someone else in their possibly lonely hours. It's a great way to counter depression and to not only be part of a network of like-minded souls, but even to create that network—like Wrong Planet[11] has done, or on a much larger scale, *Star Trek*.

Pay attention to those sparks of creativity. Don't let them pass by and don't try to medicate them away. They are little cries from the subconscious telling you to express yourself. They might hold the key to better health, more happiness and a sense of self-worth. They may also point the way to your career.

▶ **Crisis** When your fear center is enlarged, as is the case for the mildly autistic (it shrinks in the severely impaired, according to the National Institute of Mental Health[12]), you have a hard time discerning real threat from imagined threat.

As a result you may get used to operating in an emotional and physical state that most non-autistics wouldn't be able to deal with for a day, much less a lifetime. You may become hyper-vigilant, in a constant state of alert like a nightwatchman on the frontier of battle. This means that we are tough. This may help us become empathetic to others' problems, but it also means we may get used to living in crisis. Having peace, friends, money, health, may be something we will always consider unattainable for ourselves, and we may find we are always in a state of striving and barely surviving. Once you realize that fear is an emotion, not necessarily a reflection of your immediate reality, you can begin to control your life better, instead of having fear control you.

▶ **Criticism** (see *Consideration for others*, *i-muscles*) This morning I woke up to a delightful message from one of my YouTube subscribers: "your makeup is hideous and so are your razored eyebrows."[13] First of all, Auntie doesn't razor her eyebrows, although they are frequently *raised* by comments like these and are probably getting perpetually stuck in "humph" position. Second of all, this guy needs to look up two things: old pics of Lucille Ball and the word *camp*. After careful consideration of about five milliseconds I deleted and blocked him. It felt so good I almost wanted a cigarette afterward.

We talked about not burning bridges, and we must learn to take criticism to a point, but look at the context, the manner it was delivered, the source, and whether this person really wants to help, or if they just want other trolls to chime in, validate his or her useless opinion and pull you down so they can all beat their chests and woot like gorillas.

Criticism can rob us of sleep if we don't process it properly: we can be guileless and easily blindsided by it, and not realize it when it happens; instead we might realize it later. And when we do sense people are mocking or directly criticizing us, we can take it to heart and can have the situation on repeat for ages…on repeat for ages…on repeat for ages.

Having said that, although criticism is better to give than to receive, receive it we must or we are not being fair and balanced in our approach to living. When someone is critical, it instantly brings us back to that lonely place where our thoughts were not wanted. We have to try not to be oversensitive, for not every piece of advice or criticism is unwarranted or comes from a mean place.

However, we are awfully adept at giving it. Professor Tony Attwood has said that females with Asperger's are the most critical beings on the planet and instead of being offended, I felt gratitude, for that explained my nature. I wasn't just a critical woman, I was behaving like a card-carrying Aspergirl! Males on the spectrum can be quite critical as well, which is why a relationship between two Aspies (whether hetero or same sex) can seem more like a human dart game than a loving arrangement.

Most criticism is at least partly warranted. If the shoe fits you don't have to wear it, but at least admit you really are a size ten.

▶ **Crush** This is a sudden infatuation with another person that may masquerade as true love. Ah, hormones are wonderful things, as are genetics, and they will fool us into baby-making at every possible turn. Early spring is usually the worst time, and just before winter, as we all want someone we can cozy up with when the weather turns cold.

"Crush" is an appropriate term, because it can be quite an overwhelming feeling when it hits, but also, you may feel "crushed" when the object of your affections shows they are decidedly disinterested. If it happens to turn out to be true love, only time and reciprocation will tell.

▶ **Cynicism and optimism** In the modern understanding of these terms, cynicism and optimism are fraternal twins, or mirror images, like Samantha and Serena in *Bewitched*, one innocent and open, the other full of dark corners and hidden perils. Either one in itself is dogmatic, half-formed, cut off from reality. In every life come dark and light experiences, moments of joy and pain, things that paid off and things that left you broke and depleted. I think a person becomes cynical when optimism has been disappointed too many times, when there have been too many darknesses, and a black shade is drawn on the window of life. The spirit needs at least a bit of light. If it doesn't get enough, it dies. And while it might look alive, it is a dry and brittle thing, not growing, just mimicking life, until it is gone completely.

Because we Aspies can start off so naïve and trusting, we are in jeopardy of falling into cynicism and thinking everything about life is bad. If you get to that point, it's always a good idea to take the day off and make a list, preferably written, of everything you have to be grateful for. Gratitude is an excellent antidote to cynicism. For every horrid event, person or circumstance in your life, surely there must be things to be grateful for. To think on those things for a while will raise the blinds and let in some much-needed light.

At the end of the day, cynicism is spiritual laziness. You give yourself license to give up, by saying that nothing matters.

D

▶ **Dating** (see *Relationships*) The road to partnership is full of potential pitfalls, and even Auntie can be myopic enough to stumble into them. Love (or at least lust) is the anesthesia nature uses to extract babies from us. As soon as we see someone we like, we see them through a rainbow-colored haze. We might say or do anything to be with them. And they might do the same. So you might not be getting a clear picture of who they are and vice versa. That's why it's a really good idea to take some time to get to know someone. If you jump in the sack too soon, you might find yourself with an unexpected passenger when you try to jump out of it. By that I mean a baby, an STD (sexually transmitted disease) or a broken heart. So try to "vet" your potential partner and go on a date with them. A good, old-fashioned date. And then more dates. Don't plan to meet someone on a Monday, move in on Wednesday and by Saturday buy cats and plant tulips; extend that to at least a year or more in the schematic of your life. And realize they not only might but will have an agenda all their own and it might not include you in it (see *Rejection*).

Some people can have sex without being in love, and others can't. Figure out which one you are and be honest about it, first and foremost with yourself. Some people approach the dating game with an earnest intent of meeting their soulmate, while others might be more in the "acquisitions and mergers" category.

We on the spectrum sometimes don't recognize or care about age disparity. Make sure they are legal, first of all, and then, that they want and are capable of providing the same sorts of things you do. It's probably time to stop being a cougar when your age spots make you look more like a leopard, but hey, if it's working for you, who is Auntie to judge?

Don't settle for the first person who wants you. Other women on the spectrum tell me the same thing: that their dating landscape resembles the back room at Good Will. The stuff nobody wants. So, how *do* you find Mr. or Ms. Right?

Aspie groups (online and in real life, or IRL), college, work—you never know where you might find someone to go out with. There are many dating sites, from the mainstream, like eHarmony, to those dedicated to subcultures like goths, farmers and raw foodies. When putting your profile together, don't confuse honesty with TMI; too much information can be a romance killer. Here's what *not* to write in your personal ad:

> Man wanted for sex, helping with bills, and doing all the chores I hate. Must be willing to sleep in the spare room when I don't want to be touched, not bother me when I'm working. You have all yer original teeth. If the hair that's supposed to be on your head is on your back, please don't call.

We have to be honest, but not too honest right off the bat. Mystery is an aphrodisiac, the excitement of the unknown. Don't lie but don't reveal all right away.

So you've got a date? Gentlemen, take a tip from Aunt Aspie. If you are interested in a woman, you have to be interested in what she does and what she likes. Especially women on the spectrum—our works define us to a large extent. Do you want an equal, or a blow-up doll, a blank slate you can impute things on? I can't tell you how many times blokes have talked over me on dates, not taking the slightest interest in what I think or do, just how cool I look in the moment. Ladies, if he's not interested in what you do then he's not interested in who you are. Run away. We have no time for time wasters, pretty boys too confident in their own looks to make an effort at character building, leeches or laziness.

Folks, try going out with someone who actually likes you and cares about you and see how that goes, instead of going for a physical type. Attractiveness is important, but nothing is more beautiful than a good heart.

Women, if you're on a date with someone, don't imagine yourself walking down the aisle with him and start naming babies in your head. He'll see a mad gleam in your eye and run for the door. Instead, *listen to and observe* the actual person in front of you. If you think being accommodating and forgiving of rudeness or any other trait is going to be rewarded, forget it. You're putting a doormat sign on your forehead. If he checks out every girl who walks past while you're talking, ask him if he wants you to get their phone numbers for him. That's not jealousy: he's being discourteous and painfully obvious about it.

A few last words: sometimes when it comes to love affairs, a fantasy should remain just that.

Don't imagine what he might be, see what he is.

▶ **Death** (see *Transitions*) When it comes to death I think we Aspies have an edge on the one hand, and a harder time on the other. We can be quite pragmatic about death, once we realize as small children that it's inevitable. So when an older relative dies, for example, or someone who was unwell or unhappy, we can be matter of fact about it.

It is sometimes also quite difficult for us to empathize with something we have not personally experienced. Our reaction may seem cold. If this is you, remember to say kind things to the friends and relatives of the deceased, like "I'm sorry for your loss." It is the polite and appropriate response to such news. (Personally, I don't like the expression "rest in peace": it sounds boring. I hope it's a blast wherever I'm going.)

The death of someone close to us can really highlight our own mortality and kindle a morbid preoccupation in a Woody Allen sort of way. Also, death is a huge transition and we all know how well Aspies adapt to those. So whether it's our own inevitable transition or the loss of someone who is part of our routine, it can be very difficult for us.

Having a belief system can be helpful, whether it's a religious one or a scientific one, although it is good to research many belief systems, from atheist to Christian to Buddhist, etc., before you ever settle on the one that feels right to you. It's also okay to admit you don't know for certain what happens after death, which in itself is very liberating. The worst thing we can do, and the families of people on the spectrum can do, is not talk about it, or not let people fully express their thoughts and feelings on the subject and on the passing of the person or pet. Those are highly potent times in a person's life and a great opportunity for growth as an individual and as a family. (For further reading I recommend Deepak Chopra's *Life After Death*.[14])

▶ **Deficits** (see *Strengths, abilities and challenges*) Work with your strengths, work on your deficits. For us to admit we have deficits is very liberating—the first step in overcoming the erroneous "if I make a mistake I *am* a mistake" mentality (see *Black and white thinking*). That seems to come as an unwanted bonus program in our ASOS (autism spectrum operating system), kind of like getting a new default browser when you download software—you didn't ask for it, it was slipped in, and it's often difficult to figure out how to get rid of it. But you can get rid of it, even if it's more like a virus.

When you admit you aren't great at something, it shows you have matured as a person and are big enough to admit you aren't omniscient. I've met many young Aspies for whom that is still unthinkable. Any deficit you have, whether it's hitting a ball with a stick, driving, doing sums, or diplomacy, if it means a lot to you, barring actual physical and mental limitations, you can use your Aspie tenacity to overcome it.

▶ **Depression** There is a difference between sadness and depression. Sadness is a reasonable and appropriate response to certain events, e.g. the death of a loved one, or the end of a love affair. Depression is a deep dark well that we fall into, which becomes physically and mentally immobilizing. It's like being swathed in a dark spirit, and was surely the true cause of countless cases of spirit possession ascribed by our ancestors and certain cultures. Depression truly feels like the end of the world, the end of all happiness and light.

Mood is a cloud covering the sun. It passes. The true state of the sky is blue and clear. Your true state of being is also clear. Do what you must to "cloudburst" or to wait it out until things are clear again. Never for one second think that the cloud is the sky.

On a personal note, I understand full well what a horrible thing depression is. Until this year, I spent more time in that well than out of it, since my early childhood. How do I manage to climb out? I spoke in *Aspergirls*[15] about taking action when we're depressed, as depression is often caused by a feeling of powerlessness to bring what we want into our lives—whether love, money, friendship, health, etc. Since then, I've discovered another antidote: giving up gluten. As bizarre as that sounds, and I know it does, it happens to be true. For me. I don't know if it will work for you. Gluten may have no discernible instant reaction so the connection goes unnoticed, but it is very possibly the cause of our inner fog. Our inner happiness, meanwhile, is running around in the fog trying to come to light, like Nicole Kidman in *The Others*, to no avail.

Some say going casein-free is equally important. If the thought of giving up cheese and dairy is still too much for you to seriously contemplate, know that we each reach our milestones when we are ready. All we can do is keep trying to go forward.

In my humble, non-medical-doctor opinion, I think the modern tendency to medicate depression is folly. In addition to making sure that the material facts of your life are positive—good job, health, friends, etc.—and if the spiritual side of your life is addressed—you spend some time believing in and practicing some form of higher love and meditation—

then I confidently suggest that diet may be the culprit, or at least part of it.

When the sad events of life wash you away from your safe and happy place, your spirit should be able to float on them and eventually swim back to shore. Having depression is like having a stone around your ankle, pulling you under, making everything seem impossible. If you are depressed, I hope you will look into healthy and natural ways *first* to ease it.

▶ **Diagnosis** (see *Asperger's: As a label, Mental illness*) I'm always hearing about some bacteria that's only found in the intestines of autistic people which might lead to an "autism blood test" or mapping of brainwaves that will prove a diagnosis conclusively. So far this has not happened so the label is still, and maybe always be going to be, fairly subjective.

People ask me quite frequently if an official diagnosis is important. For school children and some employees there can be real and tangible consequences to having or not having that paper. My beliefs are this—on one hand, the DSM and other diagnostic manuals are western constructs. On the other hand, a diagnosis gives you a frame of reference to explain your qualities and experiences. It gives you a community to talk to and learn from, inspire and be inspired by. It also gives you a body of work to read, view or listen to.

Despite my own ambivalence, I was generally happy and relieved to have the validation of the diagnosis. Many of us frame them and hang them on our walls. But like the *Doctor of Thinkology* certificate given to the scarecrow by the Wizard of Oz, it's more what the paper represents and means to you than it having any intrinsic value.

Whether or not you have an official diagnosis, if the information helps, use it!

▶ **Diagnostic and Statistical Manual (DSM)** Currently in its fifth edition, this is the American Psychiatric Association's (APA) classification and diagnostic tool.[16] It is used by doctors and psychologists in the United States and in at least 65 other countries to diagnose autism and mental illness.

▶ **Diet** (see *Depression, Eating disorders, Gastrointestinal issues*) Telling someone to change their diet can be as incendiary a topic as religion or politics. However, it is strongly recommended by many that people on the spectrum avoid gluten, chemicals and monosodium glutamate (MSG), and some say also soy, and casein, found in dairy. We all have different dietary needs, based on lifestyle, medical problems and more, but I think it's safe to say modern living may give us a lot of choices and they aren't necessarily the healthiest ones.

Many people today do not eat a wide variety of *fresh* food, especially vegetables. The only veggies they get are the flaccid leaves of iceberg lettuce to be found in a fast-food burger. Consequently, although they may be overweight they may be malnourished. If you succumb to seductive commercials and time constraints, and get a fast-food burrito, take a moment to really taste it—you may discover it actually tastes like dog food. To think that millions of children are eating this kind of stuff daily is heartbreaking. Make your own: rice, beans, meat, fresh guacamole (with garlic and lime), red leaf lettuce, homemade salsa with heirloom tomatoes, green onion, fresh cilantro, all on a gluten-free tortilla. This is just one of a million delicious alternatives to fast food you can make at home.

A vegetable garden isn't as hard to grow as you may think. In addition to providing healthy, vitamin-rich veggies far fresher than what you get at your supermarket, it can save you a lot of money over time. If something doesn't flourish, replace it with what does. Even if you live in a high rise, you can grow plants from pots or a hanging shoe organizer on your balcony.

Instead of spraying your lawn with chemicals, let it go organic. After a few seasons the dandelions will be safe to eat. They are a delicious superfood. Cook with garlic and crushed red pepper, and toss with gluten-free pasta and Parmesan cheese for pure heaven!

Meats should be unprocessed, organic and free range, but of course many of us can't afford that. If you look around, there may be a farm (or farmer's market for you city-dwellers) somewhere nearby that sells seasonal offerings of their own livestock, cut and packaged. Same with eggs. A Sunday walk or drive may lead you to discover a farmhouse with a cardboard sign advertising eggs. Those home-grown items are usually cheaper and tastier than store bought ones.

Avoid processed, chemical-laden foods. You wouldn't put sugar in your gas tank, don't put junk in your tank! Your supermarket checkout should resemble and represent the kinds of foods nature provided for us, not some CEO and Madison Avenue advertising exec.

Food allergies are another consideration. Quite often we become addicted to the very things we should be avoiding.

Some say that naturally fermented foods are a necessary part of any diet, to create the right balance of intestinal flora, which is especially necessary in our case. (Read *The Body Ecology Diet* by Donna Gates.[17]) Many also say that food combining is the key to optimum health and weight. This is also discussed in Gates's book. You can read about it on the Body Ecology website.[18]

Finding the right diet may be the single most important thing you can do to minimize the unpleasant aspects of AS. I encourage you to read more on gluten-free, casein-free and other autism-friendly diets. Look for some books on my website.

▶ **Disability** I've always disliked this word. To me "disability" is like a big fat armchair you fall into and can never get out of; all you can do is change the channel on your TV with the remote and shout for someone to bring you snacks from the kitchen. I have met some people who called themselves disabled and made excuses all day about why they couldn't do things, instead of focusing on what they could do.

Asperger's does define and limit you to some extent, but it also gives one the depth and abilities to circumvent those limitations, just as any disability brings heightened abilities in other areas if we look for them, e.g. the blind person with the keen sense of hearing or smell.

I prefer to use the term *diffability* when describing AS. It's corny, but it's far less victimizing and much more accurate a term.

If you have disabilities in addition to AS, as many of you do, you may feel that you have been dealt a very unfair hand in life. It's not the hand you're dealt, it's the sportsmanship with which you play it. Most people on the spectrum I've met who bear additional burdens have been incredibly gracious and generous people. It is through adversity we forge real character.

▶ **Discipline and organization** (see *Executive function*)
These can be problem areas for us, especially as we get older. Even if you used to be a champion multi-tasker, life gets more complicated and memory more overloaded. What follows are some ideas to help you. If you are incapable, you are in need of closer support than some of us. If you are a support person, you may have to be the one to create some simple lists for your charge. It's one aspect of AS that can be debilitating and humiliating and you can seem inconsiderate of other people too if you can't remember to pay bills or pick up groceries or even your child.

- Try making lists or writing things down:

    ○ Use a whiteboard to write down tasks for the day, and printouts hung on a cork board for longer-term projects.

    ○ Weekly job charts are good for keeping a clean house. E.g. Monday is laundry day, Tuesday vacuuming, etc.

    ○ Keep a list of things by the door you need to take with you when you leave your house: wallet, phone, keys, water, that sort of thing.

- For problems with getting lost:

  - If you travel outside your home you must have GPS in your car or on your phone or tablet.

  - If you don't have any of these, print maps out before leaving. Include maps of buildings or campuses as well as routes there.

- A mix-and-match wardrobe does wonders for getting Aspie junior and senior off to school or work on time.

- A cell phone is a must for those of us who tend to be late, or who are fearful of going to new places.

- Viewing images or videos of places we are going to in advance can help orient us once we are there and save us getting lost/wasting time.

- A simplified household, with little clutter and places where things "live" when not in use, is also helpful.

- Eating brain foods like omega-3s and not doing drugs or drinking too much will keep the mind sharper longer.

▶ **Disclosure** If you are newly diagnosed, you may be wondering if, when and how to disclose. You may want to tell everyone you meet, but there's a time and a place. Telling the cashier you underestimated your total because you are dyscalculic is probably unnecessary. If you're on the dance floor and the bass is pounding and a beautiful girl sidles up, it may not be the best time to say you have proprioception issues and will try not to step on her feet. Not that it's something to be ashamed of; it will just be jarring and confusing. However, if you are having AS-related issues at work and wish to keep your job for a long time, then you have to think about disclosure. Or, if you are on a second date with someone and really like them.

Every situation may call for a different option. You may never have to tell your boss because you're managing fine, or you may not have to if you are obviously affected. You can partially disclose—e.g. ask to make changes that you need—without spelling out that you have AS. Once you open that door, you can't close it, so do think carefully about your options.

With so many things in life, it ain't what you say, it's the way that you say it. Looking away, meekly uttering with hunched shoulders "I have Asperger's so I can't _____ (fill in the blank)" is not going to work very well. Let's take the work example. Ask your boss for five minutes of her time. Start a conversation with something positive, whether it's work-related or whatever. It must be sincere. Then, matter-of-factly state how much you love your job and appreciate working there. Follow it with "I'd like to ask a small favor," and segue into a short list of requests. Make sure you've narrowed it down to a couple of sentences. You can tell her you have Asperger's, or you can simply mention the trait/stimulus that is causing the issue, e.g. "Fluorescent lights give me headaches. My doctor recommends turning them off over my desk and using a standing lamp." Who could argue with that?

On a date or with a new friendship, I like to take a humorous approach. "If I see you unexpectedly, I might not recognize you right away. I'm not senile, I have prosopagnosia—face blindness. So don't break up with me, just walk up and re-introduce yourself." Or, "If I wear earplugs when we hang out, it's not that I'm not interested in what people are saying, I just hear ten when they think their volume switch is at two." (Seriously though, don't you dislike shouters? The people who are orating for Carnegie Hall when they're sitting in the front seat of their Mini and you're trapped in there with them?)

These are partial forms of disclosure. Whether or not you choose to use the words *autism spectrum* or *Asperger's* is your business and no one else's.

When young children are involved, it is the parents' decision. The media really screwed up the use of the word Asperger's over the last few years. Honestly, if I were a parent of a school-age child on the spectrum I'd be livid and I'd be conflicted. Asperger's became a catch-all at both ends—the media dishing out the label and some doctors and counselors handing out the diagnosis to everyone not fitting in. I'd stick with partial disclosure and, if I had to, autism spectrum. Parents, if you need admin support and an Individualized Education Program (IEP) it will vary from school to school in how effective it is and how it is dealt with.

The fact of the matter is, the more normal you appear the less likely you will be taken seriously. I and my spectrum friends have heard all sorts of nonsense, even from doctors: "You look too normal, too intelligent, too this, not enough that." When that happens, ask, "Oh really? What do people with Asperger's look like?" These same people then proceed to get perplexed, upset or even angry when we act in a way that is inconsistent with so-called normal non-autistic behavior. Sometimes I think I'll get a red "A" tattooed on my scalp so I could part my hair like Damien in *The Omen* and show them my mark.

A succinct, polite disclosure might be "I'm on the autism spectrum which means I have a neurological difference that makes certain things you do seem really stupid and like a foreign language to me, mostly in the social and sensory but also in the cognitive arena."

As for the benefits, well, for every benefit you gain by telling you'll probably lose another. And I can guarantee that no matter how many times you tell someone you have Asperger's, they still won't get it unless they're one of those Aspie-friendly, Aspie-*curious* people who are truly interested in understanding. Many people will think they understand because they saw some movie and feel shy once in a while. Eventually they'll say things like "Can't you just _____?" or "Isn't there medication for that?"

We all have challenges in life. Some people may actually resent that yours has a name and literature. When you label yourself, you risk alienating others. Since you have probably been alienated yourself you might not care now, but at the end of the day, we all have more in common than we don't.

▶ **Do-it-yourself (DIY)** People on the spectrum tend to be very self-sufficient as a matter of lifelong coping and survival. While we can learn myriad things through books, YouTube and formal education, and be true Jacks-and-Jills-of-all-trades, if not renaissance people, it is part of life to learn that we all need the help of others from time to time, whether it be a doctor, contractor or plumber. You will learn your limitations and you will learn to reach out to others when necessary. In some cases, a penny saved is a penny earned, but in other cases, you're better off hiring a pro right from the beginning. In the case of medical problems, it's all well and good to think you can cure your own disease, but it never hurts to get medical tests and a second qualified opinion.

▶ **Doctor visits** During the end of the writing of this book, I was diagnosed with some serious issues. Like many of my AS friends, I abhor doctor visits. I dislike waiting rooms, cold instruments, gruff doctors, fluorescent lights, medical bills, and so on. Rather than subject myself to regular checkups, I avoided them altogether, thinking that what I didn't know couldn't hurt me. I am now facing further treatment, suggested surgery (which I will do everything in my healing power to not require) and a lifelong lifestyle and dietary change. I implore you to get over your aversion. If you get claustrophobic in waiting rooms, hate people touching you and so on, think how much of that you will have to deal with if you let some minor thing become serious by not getting checkups.

Here in the States, I had the added difficulty of not being able to afford the three hundred dollar plus per month that I was asked to pay for basic insurance, and it wasn't until Obamacare forced my hand and my income had decreased to the point where I was provided with free health insurance, that I finally got some. For my UK and other friends, this won't be an issue, but for some Americans and others, it still might be. It's worth searching out "pay-what-you-can" clinics, such as they have in many cities, like San Francisco Womens' Community Clinic.

Whether you want to disclose during a doctor visit is up to you. I once asked a dentist for a squeeze toy that he had for children, telling him that I had Asperger's. He replied with, "I'm used to all sorts of loonies." That may have been the beginning of my aversion to doctor visits. Bring your own cuddle toys and sensory kit. Exercises like yoga and martial arts will help you learn to relax your body enough to allow a doctor to examine you, but you need to integrate them into your daily life for a while before you see benefits that you can call up when you need to. If you need to wear colored sunglasses or whatever while you're being examined, a good doctor won't mind and certainly won't mock you for it. If they do, I'd suggest finding a different doctor. A good one, like a good teacher, is a beautiful thing. A bad bedside manner can really scar a person for life; don't allow yours to do that to you. Find a better one! They are out there.

Please do remember that doctors have come through the ranks of a particular educational system. They may not have the big picture, or holistic leanings. The tendency to medicate and perform surgery without exhausting other possibilities is rampant in the West. At the very least, get a second opinion before giving up organs or going against your gut instincts.

▶ **Drinking to cope** (see *Substance abuse*) Drinking to cope with the social anxiety or challenges that come with ASDs is no better than drinking to cope with anything. If you can have a nightcap without wearing the whole set of pajamas, you should be fine. Moderation is key. If you cannot moderate your behavior, either because of extremist tendencies, going through a very bad patch, or genetic predisposition to alcoholism, then you'd best avoid it. The only thing worse than a meltdown is a drunken autistic meltdown.

E

▶ **Eating disorders** (see *Body image*, *Diet*) Many people on the spectrum, especially women, have experienced eating disorders at some point in their lives.

First of all, most experts say, and I agree, that autism starts in the gut—we have enlarged pores in our gastrointestinal tract, a "leaky gut" that allows elements in food to pass into the bloodstream and brain that would normally be broken down and excreted. Instinctively, we as Aspie children may feel we're not eating what we should and may reject most or all food because of this. We may also crave the very things that harm us—the drug that makes us feel good for a while which perpetuates the cycle of addiction and decline.

Eating "non-foods" as a child is a hallmark of autism, which explains my early penchant for paper, especially the sticks that hold the lollipop—suck on them long enough and they unfurl into a sweet papery treat. I also spread Elmer's glue on my hand the way some people spread jam, then would peel it off and eat it with the same delight. Coins and other metal objects were also delicious, and I loved to put handfuls of them in my mouth and suck on them, or lick metal poles. (I learned pretty quickly not to do that in winter.) Unfortunately I also learned that paper was made from wood, and couldn't resist swallowing a toothpick which resulted in a quick trip to the doctor where I had to have it removed with forceps. You or your child may have similar appetites which lead to similar predicaments. There are many reasons for this: sensory preference; not knowing the difference between foods and non-foods; and malnutrition, meaning that kids are not getting what they need from their diet.

A nutritionist, if you can afford one, would be a good start, but you can also use some research and common sense. Where the metal is concerned, it shouldn't have been difficult to tell that I perhaps needed some iron or zinc in my diet. Eating paper may indicate a desire for starch, for I remember finding holy wafers and other papery foods delicious and grew to love rice and pasta (fortunately discovering gluten-free). Beyond these things, I'd be very strict as to what I would eat. Bologna on cheap white bread mainly. Canned, salty soup, deplorable things to give any child. A whole grain diet with pulses, unprocessed meats, vegetables of a wide variety and fruits is the way to go and will prevent or combat obesity in most cases, barring other causes. Some say a healthy autism-friendly diet also consists of naturally fermented foods (read *The Body Ecology Diet*[19]). It is better to get a small amount of good food than a larger amount of crap.

I've had verbal wrestling matches with moms whose autistic kids will only eat fast food. I've seen young people with evidence of food allergies craving the exact foods that they seem allergic to. Telling someone that eating the food they love is killing them is a bit like telling a giant toddler with a bat that there's no Santa Claus; be warned, it can get ugly. Changing your diet takes a bit of effort to retrain the mind and the taste buds but it mostly certainly can be done, with patience, perseverance and experimentation. Once you do, you'll never go back to Ding Dongs with the same relish ever again.

Anorexia and bulimia When we get a little older the eating disorders may take one of these forms. (I did not escape, having both throughout my teens and early twenties.) Of course, anorexia can set off years of poor metabolism, resulting in weight fluctuations, bulimia to counteract those, and ill health due to malnutrition, from chronic bronchitis to a generally ravaged digestive system.

Here are some theories as to why we develop eating disorders, though these reasons may not apply to you and yours:

- Some parents don't really know how to communicate with their children and vice versa. Rejection of a parent's food may be a cry for help, for understanding, a way to say, "Don't you see what's happening with me? I need to talk!" Literally, although we may not quite realize it at the time, a hunger strike.

- Anorexia and bulimia may be the result of a skewed body image, extreme anxiety and also a desire for control—especially when we're teenagers. School, parents, jobs, acne, puberty, we have very little control over our lives and bodies, so this may be one way to exert some.

- Gastrointestinal issues that make eating problematic are already making digestion abnormal. Starving ourselves may be one way to avoid some of the pain and suffering we know we will endure.

- Bulimia can be a kind of perseveration—cook, eat, throw up so that you can do it all over again.

There *is* a lot of bad food in the world that we should naturally reject. But there's a lot of good food too. You can learn to love feeding your body natural food, especially if you grew it yourself or it was grown/raised by local farmers. We must learn to love food. Your brain and your spirit need it. You do not have to starve to be slim if that's your concern. It's a question of slowly re-educating yourself. Once you understand the difference between fresh whole foods and canned mush, you'll never touch the latter again. Sorry British friends, canned mushy peas are probably the nastiest things I've ever encountered, right up there with spam and fluffernutter. Avoid nearly all packaged, processed foods as if it were poison because a lot of it is. Think of yourself as a fine vessel (I won't say *Titanic*) and fast-food restaurants as the iceberg that can sink you. Use good restaurants as an occasional treat, for even the best tend to use far too much salt and fat and serve too-large portions, and avoid too much meat or deep-fried stuff.

Eat like your life depends on it…because it does.

▶ **Echophenomena (echolalia, palilalia and echopraxia)** *Echolalia* is the repetition of words and phrases uttered by another, while *palilalia* is repeating yourself. *Echopraxia* is imitating someone else's actions.

Imitating, emulating physical and verbal actions, is how we primarily learn (up to the age of two or three), but when these behaviors become reactions rather than a means for learning, they are considered echophenomena. How one is certain it is reactive and not learning in progress is sure to be a grey area—an actor may display these sorts of tendencies for life, since they are ever studying other people's body language and dialect—and it is impossible to tell by age three or four exactly what the motivation may be.

Echophenomena are not exclusive to autism, and are found in Tourette's and other conditions. I was highly echolalic as a child. For me, a word, a phrase, was like a piece of music, a one-word poem, whose utterance enriched my soul and enraptured my mind. In my case, it was closely linked to my love of and future career with words and music. Such may not be the case with you: they may merely be soothing mechanisms. I had an Aspie aunt who used to repeat words and phrases many times and then giggle. Her favorite was "myocardial infarction." She was an English teacher with a love of the language.

Echophenomena seem harmless enough in their milder states, although they may certainly be debilitating to the sufferer and jarring for other people in their more extreme forms. If you are an adult with a propensity to echolalia, perhaps there is some budding or latent creativity. Maybe it is a soothing mechanism and you can replace it with a more socially acceptable one. There are many activities that require repetition that you might find satisfying. Echolalia is also a way to memorize things, to file them away in long-term memory, the way a song is used to teach the alphabet to youngsters. With classically autistic people, it may be used to respond to a question they do not know they answer to: for example, answering the question "Where are you?" with the same question. The mind may be searching for the right answer but doesn't have it within its grasp. Or answering "Did you brush your teeth?" with the same question if the answer is "No" but they know they were supposed to, so therefore "No" should not be uttered. So echolalia can indicate stress. With higher-functioning individuals, it will more likely be a stress reliever. If it is compulsive and debilitating, if you cannot control it or replace it, you may need some behavioral therapy.

▶ **Education** The happiest Aspies I know are those who are working in their field of passion, especially in an academic environment, lecturing about and sharing their passions with the next generation. Whether you are an engineer, anthropologist, librarian, or a million other interesting things, you will have one thing in common—a degree in something. Having a degree these days cannot guarantee you a good income. But not having one almost certainly does limit monetary success. I should know. Aunt Aspie is one of the few writers in this field who is self-educated and it has impacted my ability to achieve the heights that others have reached. I thought that after all the books I've written, somebody would give me an honorary degree. The only degree I get is the third degree… "Where'd you go to school, who diagnosed you, how'd you write those books when you don't have a PhD?" (I do have an MFA but it doesn't stand for anything I can say here.)

I've written about this at length, but there are a couple of points I'd like to make here in addition: First, don't bite off more than you can chew. Just because your brain can handle a double major doesn't mean the rest of you can. You still have to think about social and sensory overload. Take your time and have downtime as often as possible to recharge.

Second, try to educate your staff about ASCs (autism spectrum conditions) if you can't attend an AS-specific program. Even dropping them a copy of *Aspergirls*[20] or *Asperger's on the Job*[21] might help.

Lastly, get as much education as you can, for your self-esteem as well as your wallet, even though loans are prohibitive in some countries. That way, even if you want to join the circus, you can still be the trapeze artist with the degree in something to provide you with the other net you might need at some point.

▶ **Eidetic and photographic memory** Temple Grandin has photographic memory. She remembers every shoe, for example, she's ever seen and can call it up "like Google for images" (her words). Eidetic memory is a short-lived version of that. The latter is quite common for spectrum dwellers I believe. It's the "tape recorder brain" that keeps us up all night, replaying the sights and/or sounds of the day. I believe it is connected to our creativity, and may be a key to our career, if used properly. For example, a girl on the spectrum goes to see *Avatar*, and when she gets home, cannot sleep until she has painted the images from memory. Or a boy attends a concert and simply must play the concerto when he arrives home, although it is midnight.

These are the fortunate kiddies that have toys, tools and instruments to "exorcise the demon" but what about the rest of us, those who do not know they have the talent, or who don't have the tools? They may lie awake all night, kicking the footboard and driving their sibling crazy, or pace the house driving Mum and Dad mad, or fall asleep at school next day because they didn't get a wink of sleep after the day trip to Manhattan. The modern need to medicate is a knee-jerk reaction to what might be a simple need for *art* and *expression*. Some of our greatest artists start out as mimics, recreating what they've seen and heard, until they get older and some unique bit of creativity, the result of all the practice they got from studying others, bursts forth.

Even if your little Sheldon or Sharon is not a budding Picasso or Mozart, maybe they have more of an athletic need—the need to dance or run or swim, or play ball. My advice is to listen to what they are mimicking or what is keeping them up at night. Ask them if they'd like to play/ write/sing/paint it out themselves, and experiment until something clicks. Be advised, however, some of us will get frustrated and give up quickly when our violin sounds more like a wounded animal than an instrument of beauty. Black and white thinking might make us think we stink. Be prepared to explain that practice is a crucial part of any art.

▶ **Emotions** What are they? Anger, sadness, fear, joy, etc. They are different than knowledge or reasoning. They, like love, can make us do silly things. They can also move mountains. This power may be precisely why so many people on the spectrum, men particularly (sorry fellas), tell me that they "can't handle emotional things." Other people's emotions may frighten or drain you, if you can't even handle or identify your own (known as *alexithymia*). The quest for emotional maturity may be a lifelong search for some of us, others may never try, preferring to shut down when things get hot and heavy. Life is about relationships and where there are other people, there are always emotions. You might as well roll up your sleeves and get used to it. Life can break you open, lay you out on a table, pick at your innards, put you back together and then say "get on with it," but that's life. You can choose to be stronger and wiser with each episode or go back into your turtle shell. If you stay there, however, you are missing out on a lot. Make friends with your emotions, and learn to handle them in a healthy way, rather than letting them handle you.

▶ **Empathy** I have a theory that Aspies are better at expressing empathy in writing, while non-autistics may be better at it in person. That's because we're better at expressing ourselves without the pressure and confusion of all the stuff coming at us when other people are around—energy, eye contact, body language, subtext, pheromones. I communicate daily with my hundreds of mostly Aspie Facebook friends, and I find them to be the kindest, most compassionate bunch of people I've ever known. The non-autistics who beat me up and tormented me daily in school were not. So I think that "Aspies lack empathy" is a myth, plain and simple. Some of us cannot watch a film in which someone falls or otherwise gets hurt without actual physical pain shooting through our bodies. Yet, if you tell us in conversation that something bad happened, we might miss it entirely, or skip right over it and talk about something else to take your mind off of it, or our mind if it made us uncomfortable.

If you are Aspie, try to allow your compassion for others to show when appropriate; it lets them know that Spock is a feeling creature after all. If you really don't feel empathy for someone's pain, take a moment to put yourself in the role of the subject; you might find your emotions engage quite quickly if it's *your* car that broke down or your pet that died.

If you aren't Aspie but love someone who is, trust me when I say that still waters can run very deep, but sometimes we're so busy trying to compute and seem normal that underneath the placid surface there is a whirlpool of roiling thoughts and emotions.

▶ **Employment and self-employment** Some cultures have no word for "work"—they merely describe what they're doing: fishing, cooking, hunting, gathering, etc. Aspies seem to be of this mindset. We love to be engaged in our special interests, and if we can get paid for it, it is the farthest thing in the world from being "work." Work is what we do in social situations—those things that make us itch and sweat and palpitate and cringe.

The hardest challenge we ever find ourselves in at work is getting along with our co-workers and bosses, so often work problems are social in nature. Three things will help you more than all others—humor, humility and *self-awareness*. If you have those, you can finagle almost any situation at work. Make people laugh and they'll love you or at least not want to punch you in the nose. Ask someone for their opinion (or their help) and seem genuinely interested and they won't think you're a smug know-it-all (because let's face it, we can be) and if you're self-aware, you'll know when to use those things, or use your sensory tools, and so on. Give us tasks and we're ducks in water. But the social thing makes work hard work.

Disclosure and accommodations are a big part of the work puzzle for some of us. I've written about this at great length in *Asperger's on the Job*.[22] In that book, you'll also find my "personal job map," a useful tool for discovering what your dream job might be, and interview tips.

Many of us will find ourselves starting our own businesses, making our own opportunities, partly because society has a tendency to confuse confidence with quality so we get left out of the hiring game. You'll have to work very hard; it takes a lot of hats to run your own business, and some of them might not be your style. You may have to be your own secretary and accountant, and do your own web design and marketing, in addition to making or providing whatever it is you do. Try to get some help when and where you can. If you wear too many hats your head might cave in from the weight of them all. Also, don't think that running your own business means you don't have to deal with people. No man is an island, even if he lives on one; you still need customers and clients, employees and suppliers. Be the kind of person *you'd* want to deal with, and watch things blossom.

Working from home: One has to be even more disciplined but there are several advantages, including not needing a dog sitter, and instead of taking breaks by the water cooler, you're able to throw in a load of wash or do the morning's dishes. Another plus is not needing a uniform (writers and hookers are two of the only professions who make money in bed, and writers are very nearly respected).

Being self-employed can be very peaceful, but it can also be a lonely business. You might find you will have more motivation to make friends and work on diplomacy skills once you've gotten over the honeymoon phase of being alone for a while.

▶ **Epiphany** is a profound realization, a true *aha*, light bulb moment. (It is not the name of a stripper although it sounds like it could be.) The brain is a flexible organ, and most people, including autistic people, will have occasional realizations their whole lives that might be considered epiphanies. It was an epiphany when I realized that I probably had Asperger's. Some epiphanies are fun, some make you feel lighter, others are unpleasant, like giving birth to a bowling ball: like when you encounter a character trait that you despise in others, then realize you possess this trait in spades. Not a very nice feeling at all, but good for growth. Epiphanies are exhausting, especially for Aspies, with their black and white thinking. Realizing you've done something less than perfectly your whole life can be regrettable, but instead, be grateful that you realize it now.

Epiphanies aren't often instantaneous. I think there's a progression: first you hear something and either don't (or don't want to) believe it, then you start to believe it because it resonates with you. Then, eventually it rises up out of you as a *knowing*.

Someone should have a baby and name her Epiphany so they can say, "I just had an epiphany and it weighed 8 pounds, 9 ounces." Or "When I had my epiphany it hurt so bad I needed an epidural."

▶ **Escapism** Ask any Aspie if they prefer fiction to nonfiction, film to documentary, and they will almost always opt for the latter. Yet, how many of us are, were, and always will be, devoted to the fictitious worlds of the Starship Enterprise, Narnia, Middle Earth, Doctor Who and other similar epic tales of life in fantasy or science fiction worlds?

From experience, I can say that the only fantasies or sci-fis that appealed to this young Aspergirl were those that seemed so realistic as to read more like a history brought to life than a creation born of the imaginative mind of a mere mortal.

Because we probably never felt like we fit in our families, communities, or species, we found liberation and hope that somewhere, in some dimension, existed our true homes. Particularly because of our black and white thinking, the good vs. evil, the clearcut delineation between good guy and bad guy, would strongly appeal. I couldn't call my classmates evil, even if they taunted me, but an orc is an orc is an orc. In addition to reading about kingdoms and planets where we longed to live, we may have created our own. One such example is my novel *Orsath*, a fantasy tale set in a distant age.[23] Many of us on the spectrum have written such novels, to varying degrees of success, but the value of the act for us is undeniable.

> **Imaginary friends** Because of a lack of real friends, some of us may have created imaginary friends also. This is a normal situation to an extent, but if that is all one has, and appears to be all one needs, it could create problems with being made fun of at school, or with forming real friendships. Parents, encourage real friendships, but cautiously, and slowly. Don't throw the child in at the deep end by insisting they attend a birthday party they don't want to go to; you never know what child has been taunting yours and how merciless it can be. (See *Friend*.)

▶ **Executive function** (see *Cognitive issues*) According to Wikipedia, executive function is an umbrella term for the management (regulation, control) of cognitive processes, including working memory, reasoning, task flexibility and problem-solving as well as planning and execution. Executive function skills vary widely in the autism community, from highly organized multi-taskers to highly disorganized people who can only do one thing at a time well. (See *Discipline and organization* for some good tips on increasing daily efficiency.)

▶ **Exercise** The health of the mind affects the body—low self-esteem, depression, elation, these all affect our posture and demeanor and have roll-on effects on our life. It also works the other way around. If you have a soft, weak, clogged, unhealthy body, you aren't going to be as clear-headed as you might like. For those of us on the spectrum, certain types of physical activity can also help us with our proprioception issues. Some of us reject physical fitness and activity, in lieu of more stationary things like video games, social media, watching movies, etc. We may leave things like sports to the non-autistics of the world, since they are usually group activities, but there are plenty of things you can do on your own, or one on one.

Body/mind integration exercises are perfect for us—yoga, tai chi, etc. *Weights, and other strength trainers* will help give you confidence and lift your physique, and also make you feel more able to meet life's challenges. *Cardio exercises* such as running or anything vigorous will help strengthen your nervous system, and help with panic attacks and the symptoms of PTSD. One of the best exercises seems to have gotten lost in our society: the ritual of dancing. It's not just for college kids with too much booze in their system. Even if you're too shy/broke/whatever to go out, turn off the news, roll back the rug, turn on some music and dance at least one night away every week. There's nothing like it—it's good for the spirit and the body.

Your body is the temple which houses your spirit and mind (you know, that hard drive that sits on your shoulders). To neglect it is almost to ensure its untimely decline. If you decide to turn your body into a lean, cut, muscle machine, it's not going to make you shallow, you aren't suddenly going to have an irresistible urge to burn your books and watch Vin Diesel movies, but you will look and feel better, more formidable. People might think twice about messing with you. Your vitality will improve, and so will your mood most likely. Meltdowns might become less frequent since you'll be burning angst in more constructive ways.

When I suggest exercise to people I often get a load of excuses. You don't have to have a lot of money or join a gym which might be anathema to you. If you have an 8" x 6" floor space available, give or take, you can exercise without even leaving your house. YouTube has tons of free exercise videos on it, virtually anything you can think of from kickboxing to belly dancing.

Things you can buy: free weights, exercise mat, Pilates ball, kick bag, stationary bike.

There are lots of tips regarding home exercise but the most important one is this: keep exercise equipment above ground (not in your basement) in a place where you'll actually use it.

Because we can tend to be a bit passionate (if not OCD) about our new interests, please beware of becoming obsessed with exercise—lifting more, losing more weight, etc. This is something that needs to be integrated into your life in a way you can live with forever, not a thing that will burn hot and fast.

▶ **Expectations** We do not do well with the pressures of expectations. We like rules and assignments. They give us parameters to work within. However, expectations are more like a weight, a pressure, to perform on schedule or on command. The kinds of expectations we dread usually have to do with work deadlines and social things, such as how to behave at social functions, especially holidays: what to cook, what presents to buy, having to be merry on command. Our struggle comes from not naturally taking to social things—we have enough difficulty gleaning from one-on-one conversations, now here's a whole social more we must live up to. Yikes.

When something is coming up in which we may be "expected" to behave a certain way, or to perform a certain task, listing what we need to do, or buy, or say may be helpful. For example, your daughter is graduating and you will be expected to attend, and to hold a party afterward. This can be a nightmare for us. *List* and *enlist*. Write out what you can do, what you need, what you can't do, and what you need help with. If you find you truly are out of your element, you might even want to delegate or hire a pro.

If you truly cannot handle or afford something, and wish to opt for ignoring the expectation altogether, you must consider the impact on others. Will you be hurting those you love or who depend on you? Can you work with them to find a mutually agreeable answer? Use your Aspie ingenuity to find solutions. Perhaps you hate the idea of Valentine's Day, but your wife doesn't. Weigh cost vs. benefit. You have a peaceful(ish) February 14, but you probably have taken some of the romance out of your marriage. Doesn't sound like it's worth it in the long run. Much of this has to do with us not liking to be told what to do. At the end of the day, we all have to serve somebody, so we might as well do it to our own advantage.

Other types of expectations have to do with deadlines. Going to sleep at night can be difficult if we are expected to be awake at a certain time. Work deadlines are another. Life is a series of deadlines. If we place too much importance on a single one, it becomes larger than life, a final stop on a one-way ticket. To further use the train analogy, think of each expectation, each deadline, as a short stop on a long train ride, and it will hopefully diminish in ominousness. Even more positively, each deadline (challenge) met takes us further along the trail, and makes us stronger individuals.

On the flip side, if we have expectations of a forthcoming event, situation or friendship, we may cling so tightly to that image that if it falls short, or is different than we'd hoped, we flail and drown. While adaptability and flexibility are not things we are known for, when it comes to this, remember: anything can happen…and it usually does.

▶ **Eye contact** So much information is contained in these windows to the soul, some of it veiled, some obvious, and deciphering what is being intentionally conveyed vs. what is really felt can be overwhelming for some of us. And that's just in one direction. In the other direction, we have to try to not wince and flinch when we look in the eyes of others as that will only confuse them: "Does she not like me; do I have spinach in my teeth; is he shifty and hiding something?"

These are the kinds of questions others may mentally ask when we don't have a normal, reciprocal gaze in conversation.

Now, I don't for a minute think that non-autistics are as good at eye contact as we are led to believe. I think shyness is rampant in society, as is social awkwardness, and eye contact is difficult even for some non-autistics. I find it's best to deal with my own issues and not worry about others'. When I greet someone, I look briefly into their eyes and smile. The smile puts a sparkle in the eyes that makes other people feel comfortable. It's pretty much that simple. I don't worry in passing exchanges what their eyes are saying, whether they like me or not. What I want to convey is that I like myself and that I like them too. That sets everyone much more at ease.

With friends and loved ones, we need to be a bit more incisive and try to glean where they're at. If you really can't tell, you can always try asking. "You seem sad to me today, am I reading you wrong?" Sometimes you will and that's part of life, but other times you will be right and you open the door to real conversation. You learn to trust your instincts once they have been proven correct a few times.

How to get better? Practice, practice, practice. You will constantly fall back into the gaze-avoidance habit of yore, but when you do, just stop, look and smile (or insert appropriate facial gesture). It gets easier with time, trust me. Tip: don't stare and don't count the number of seconds you are making eye contact. Just look, make an apt facial gesture and look away. You can get away for several moments if not minutes sans eye contact as long as you occasionally repeat the three steps. If you have difficulty with facial expression you can practice with pictures and apps that will help. These are some of the things that generally do get better with age, as with age comes experience.

Another tip: if you absolutely cannot make eye contact, don't stare at the spot between or above the eyes. Look just below, at the lower lash area. I've tried this on hundreds of people and they cannot tell that I'm not looking them in the eye. Very handy when giving talks at large conferences and engaging strangers.

F

▶ **Face blindness** (see *Prosopagnosia*)

▶ **Facial expression** Recently a stranger in a pub told me to smile more. I told him to talk less. Lack of facial expression is another hallmark of autism, especially when we're young. Think of it as free Botox. It'll take that much longer for us to get crow's feet and laugh lines. I'm (mumble) years old and have my first little lines here and there. Many of us grew up studying comics, actors and models to learn how to be expressive, funny, sexy, etc. We can mimic, but quite naturally have more neutral, placid expressions. We do carry around a lot of anxiety, however, so we may scowl without being aware of it: what is sometimes referred to as "bitchy resting face." Meditation and other forms of mind–body exercise are great ways to find and project a more positive image. But telling someone to smile is a weird and bossy thing to do. We can't be pleasant on command; it's better to actually say something that makes us want to smile.

When it comes to the facial expressions of others, these take a bit of getting used to. Eye contact is difficult for us, but you will need to make cursory eye contact to tell if someone is relating to you in conversation. You will have to look at someone's face when you speak to them, to glean how well you are being understood and received. Some facial expressions will be easy to read for most of us—a grimace, a scowl, a squint, a smile. But not always. Sometimes these things are in jest, are masking other emotions, or are unrelated to what we are saying. For example, a person may scowl because they are having a stomach pain at that moment and it has nothing to do with you. When in doubt, ask. I had a colleague, a drummer, who scowled constantly when he played. I had to ask him why and he told me that's his drumming face, so I didn't take it personally.

As with most things, there are apps for our devices that help. Understanding facial expression can become an anthropological interest for some of us and, like everything else, if we choose to we can get pretty good at mastering it.

▶ **Fame** It is tempting to think, and many people do, that if we become famous, we'll finally have the upper hand and everyone will treat us with the respect we deserve. If fame were such a panacea so many of our best actors, artists and musicians wouldn't be dying so young. Mix fame with sensitivity and more money than Midas, throw in a hectic social and work schedule, travel, insomnia and possible addiction problems and you've got a recipe for one big, hot mess.

Fame does not cast an impenetrable glass bubble around you. Rather it throws open the door for all kinds of people who want a piece of you, who want to hitch a ride on your star, even if it is just a helium balloon in disguise. Fame also doesn't guarantee money or friends. Even if riches come, and it would be nice to own a larger, cushier piece of the planet to reside on, you'll still be you, just with a slightly better view.

▶ **Family dysfunction** All families have their problems, but when these problems are chronic, deep-seated and unaddressed, the term *dysfunctional* may apply. For a quiet, sensitive, thinking spectrum child, it's very difficult to behave like the sane person you were born to be, when you're swimming in a sea of dysfunction. Dysfunctional behavior is unpredictable, volatile, sometimes violent and it colors the world of a small child, autistic or not. If you were born into a dysfunctional family, you had a difficult start in life, but it can build character and instill compassion in a person. It can also inspire a lifelong quest for self-improvement. And we can improve. Be warned that if you begin to succeed in your quest, the more mentally healthy you get, the more dysfunctional people will try to twist your words and actions into something their program can understand.

In most societies and religions, children are taught to honor their parents, but if the parents are cruel or neglectful, this causes a lot of confusion and self-loathing in a child who is born a clean slate and who just wants to be loved. My brother and my sisters and I have been playing what I call *idiot soccer* ever since we were kids, kicking the ball (blame, recrimination) angrily at each other and ourselves, like deranged fools, while my mom smilingly guards the net snapping her gum like a '50s teenager because she knows we'll never kick the ball at her. Her husband is the referee, calling foul if we so much as try. I finally decided to stop playing this game after my sister died an early death from a life of alcohol and pill abuse. We can only be responsible for our own mental health and our own reactions to others (and, to some degree, our children's mental health). If people want to engage with you, they'd better play honestly and fairly, or simply excuse yourself from the game.

You can try to get your family to read about Asperger's to get to understand you better. You can lead a horse to a library but you can't make him read. Even if he reads, he'll forget most of it. There is often apathy and presumption within families ("I don't need to read about you, I lived with you") which means our families may be the last people in the world to understand us. And since Asperger's tends to run in families with related conditions that share traits with AS, the whole stew gets even more complicated.

Genes are not synonymous with loyalty and honesty. I think that, as painful as it may be to admit, some families will come round in the end, and others won't. Some of us may end up estranged from our birth families or certain members. While I'm a big one for forgiveness, without admission and atonement, the other party will probably just continue on the way they always have. It isn't wise to waste your whole life trying to make people love you who never will, trying to communicate with those whose words are poisonous to you. Best we can do in that scenario is wish them well and find a new, healthier "family," either groups of friends who love and support one another, or eventually create our own brood. If the latter, of course we may end up bringing some of that dysfunction into the next generation.

A lot of soul-searching, self-help and counseling may be in order to prevent that happening.

▶ **Forgiveness and memory anomalies** We on the spectrum can forgive and forget easily, sometimes too easily. This is a conundrum I discussed with friends. My friend Jennifer St. Jude put it better than I ever could:

> I suspect it has to do with the image in our minds. I find we put together an image of people. Often mean people present a nicer image at first as part of their learned friend/victim-making manipulation. When suddenly they act mean we see it as an inconsistent anomaly. We are happy to purge all anomalies when they cease. We Auti/Aspies hate anomalies. We are happy to see the person return to the original image. The danger in this is that we are very forgiving—a trait appreciated by the occasionally screwing up human. However, we are often exploited by the manipulating narcissist who is a master at acting badly then projecting the good image to lure us back. We are very "here and now" beings. If you're good right now you are all good. If you're bad right now you're all bad. We Spectrumites do not think collectively. We think concretely. So for us to think collectively we must utilize our secondary pattern-seeking skills. We must have many experiences of good/bad with you. Then we must have enough to formulate a pattern. When the pattern finally shows an abusive trend we will wait one more round for our other skill, fairness. But once it's been proven beyond a shadow of a doubt, you will be cut out permanently…

unless you exhibit pattern alterations. When you do that we think you've *changed!* Yikes...until after 44 years we finally learn the information that the only way a person changes is through major intervention. So if they're not in major therapy, working some program or studying healing, chances are they haven't healed, they have learned to manipulate *differently*. Here's a tip: Trust your gut all the way! For years I believed I had no instincts. Now I realize I have great instincts, I just ignore them!

We tend to have trouble keeping a person at arm's length. We can ignore them for a while, but when we interact with them again later at some point, we let them completely in. It's like we don't have that filter. Any distance seems to be dictated by the other party, and we accommodate. So either we have to keep them completely out or completely in. This frustration leads to burning bridges.

One should be good at forgiving but not forgetting. I can forgive almost anyone almost anything, but there has to be an admission of wrongdoing. There can be no forgiveness without admission and atonement. There can be no healing without dealing.

▶ **Freaks, geeks and the art of being uncool** (see *Normal*) I once wrote a song called "Kill the Cult of Cool" which, strangely, was embraced by one of the coolest DJs in Britain. Similarly, Devo sang, "we're through being cool" while wearing plant pots on their heads (I never could figure that out). Yet we may actually just want to redefine what's considered cool. And the definition changes from one generation to the next. I think it's wonderful to be unique, to be the black sheep, but if you begin to expect ostracizing and rejection, that will be self-fulfilling. Wear your geekiness with pride and a sense of belonging. You have every right to exist, just as you are.

▶ **Friend** (see *Escapism: Imaginary friends*) What is a friend, exactly? Someone with like interests? Someone you can talk to about your problems? Someone who will do things you like to do? Someone with whom there is some sort of chemistry: an unspoken, inexplicable bond? I like to think I understand what a friend is, but I suppose I'm still learning. A big part of the friend equation is being the kind of friend you want. When I was younger, friends were people who fit the above criteria, but I wasn't too concerned about the reverse. I felt like I was the star and everyone else was an extra in my play. I'm not proud of this, but it's how I felt from as far back as I can remember. For my part, I was a loyal friend, but there was still something missing: a symbiotic flow.

It takes both emotion and effort to be a friend. It doesn't mean you have to call someone every day, but you do have to call them once in a while, and not just wait for them to reach out to you. An absence of some effort in this area will result in friendships fading away. That might suit for a while, and plenty of people on the spectrum are very happy with their own company most of the time, but there comes a time in virtually everyone's life when they might need a friend. If all of yours have vanished into the mist, you might find yourself truly alone when you don't want to be.

Some people can be friends with people they hardly ever see, but autistics tend to blow so hot and cold that if we're not obsessed with someone, or someone isn't useful to us, we may feel we don't need them, and we don't need them needing us.

Because we're perfectionists, we may become disillusioned when someone shows us a flaw, or we disagree, or they make a mistake. Yet everyone makes mistakes, eventually.

If someone gets too familiar do you hyperventilate, retreat, get defensive? Find excuses for not picking up the phone? I have burnt many a bridge because I felt someone wasn't treating me with the respect I deserve or because they were acting "too familiar"…but maybe they just weren't putting me on a pedestal, maybe they were just being themselves. I'll never know. I do know that when I am about to shut someone out, I stop now and ask myself why.

Perhaps creating some sort of map or diagram would be helpful: your inner circle and then larger concentric circles to show who's where. It might also help reconcile that some family members, while related to you by blood, are not your friends. Maybe you can put them in their own adjacent or nearby circle. We can then have a set of rules and behaviors toward people in each section of the diagram: for example, "He's a close acquaintance. Always be polite, be friendly, but don't be too personal because he'll take it as an open door to the inner circle." Imagery, diagrams, can be very helpful in situations like these so that we don't suffer guilt or confusion.

Sometimes we lose friends not of our own choice but because we may say the wrong thing at the wrong time and bruise feelings. Remember that bluntness and opinions can sometimes be unwelcome visitors in a conversation. Tact and diplomacy are two of the most useful skills when developing friendships.

After years of not really getting the friend thing, I decided that I wanted friends. I'm learning how to accept the friendship of others and to give mine, without agenda or reason, other than the enjoyment of having kind and interesting people who care about me and whom I care about. It's taken me a long time, but I finally get it. Yet another example of how the autistic/Aspie brain can learn, grow and change. I used to think it was only useful to have friends who had very similar interests as myself and who could help further my career. I have since learned that I don't care to have friends in high places. I'm much more concerned about kindness and honesty.

▶ **Fun** The thing we adults and even children on the spectrum can forget to have. Try some today.

G

▶ **Gastrointestinal issues (leaky gut)** It's widely believed among scientists and experts that the person predisposed to autism has compromised or damaged pores in their gastrointestinal (GI) tract, and that "environmental insults" leak through these pores into the bloodstream and then impact brain development at an early age (in the womb, in infancy, or in early childhood) and this may be the cause of the actuation of autism.

This *leaky gut* stays with us throughout our lives (unless we take drastic concerted steps to heal it), and so GI issues remain problematic. Most people on the spectrum do have gut issues, from acid reflux to diverticulitis. Many of us have or have had irritable bowel syndrome (IBS), ulcers and more since childhood. And when we are children, we don't realize that this kind of suffering isn't normal and that it can be healed. In addition, leaky gut is continually allowing things to get into the bloodstream and impact the brain and mood throughout our lives. The only solution is to change the diet and heal the gut.

Gluten-free diet It's been mentioned in several entries in this book that a gluten-free diet can work. Gluten is found in a number of grains including wheat, barley and rye. People with celiac disease are gluten intolerant but it is also thought to be bad for autistics, both for "leaky gut" reasons, but also because the peptides in gluten may act as a drug—they pass through the walls of the compromised intestinal tract and act on the brain as an opiate, a kind of morphine if you will.

Many autistics seem to be addicted to breads, pastas and the like, and although the connection may not be made immediately, those foods may be linked to the chronic fog and depression many of us feel. On a personal note, I gave up gluten a year ago and have noticed a remarkable difference in my mood. My guts are still healing and I'm taking steps to find my way.

Casein-free diet Casein, or dairy, is meant to have the same effect, and it is recommended that a person on the spectrum eat a GFCF—gluten-free *and* casein-free—diet. Towards the end of the writing of this book, I reduced casein drastically and noticed a further clearing of my mental fog.

While this is still largely anecdotal, the results of eating an autism-friendly diet are significant and the reports substantial. I'd suggest reading about it (look for books on my website[24]) and trying an autism-friendly diet for *several months* to see if it works for you. There is a likelihood of going through a rough patch as your system gets used to doing without wheat and cheese, what's known as a healing crisis, and it may take some getting used to gluten-free versions of bread, pasta, crackers, cakes, pizza and pancakes—all of which, by the way, can be found at most major American supermarkets now. There are some truly delicious versions and some nasty ones. Some of my favorite brands are: Bob's Red Mill for terrific pancake, bread and pizza dough mix; Rudi's breads (freezer section); Udi's muffins; and DeBoles' pastas, especially the Jerusalem artichoke variety. Some of these gluten-free products are very expensive, but they tend to be heartier, especially the bread; you'll find one slice is like two normal ones. It's never easy to change your diet but some say that the cause of the rise in autism is the spread of the western diet, and the cure is in eating the right food.

▶ **Gender issues** (see *Identity*, *Sexism*) Many of us spectrumites don't feel particularly "of" our gender. Definitions of female and male can be polarizing, limiting and simply outside the realm of our thinking. I'm not talking necessarily about sexual preference, merely the way one sees themselves. If you have had concerns about this, know that it is normal for us, that there is nothing wrong with you. Identifying as a thinking, feeling, sentient being is more than enough to start with. How "feminine" or "masculine" you want to go will unfold over time. Some of us will experiment with gender identity over the years.

For outsiders, this androgyny can make the female on the spectrum seem quite tomboyish and independent, and mask the emotional fragility that might exist under the surface. Men on the spectrum can give the appearance of being very soft, gentle and quiet. The autistic mind has often been called a very "male mind" in literature. So males on the spectrum, too, can surprise over time with this seeming dichotomy.

Right from early childhood, females are told "girls should know better," and to "act like a lady." Males are told to "man up" and a lot of other seemingly innocuous phrases that are actually loaded with pressures and restrictions. With puberty comes a whole other set of responsibilities, weights, pressures and expectations. Most of these will seem pretty alien and unwelcome to Aspies. We don't care about gender in the same way that our non-autistic friends seem to, we don't seem to welcome the limiting stereotypes that come with labels. But then again, we may find that if we want to attract a partner, especially of the opposite sex, we almost have to buy into the trappings, the myths.

Femininity We can dress like women and act like women, but a lot of it will be just that—an act. Recently I was talking to my sister about a situation and she said, "Use your feminine wiles." I had to laugh. My wiles department is empty. There's a bald, one-armed, naked manikin in the corner but little else. Potential non-autistic partners may have a very hard time reading us, and while they may be attracted to our intelligence and independence, the dichotomies of AS may cause them great frustration in the end.

Society does not help portray femininity in a positive light; indeed the very word *feminist* was equated with *man-hater* in the 1970s and has pretty much remained there. Society would rather see us as hair-curling, lipstick-wearing connivers and corrupters. Look at some recent television series titles: *Devious Maids*, *Mean Girls*, *Pretty Little Liars*, *Desperate Housewives*; there are many more I don't want to know about. Even when the baddies are portrayed as such, and often get what's coming to them, it doesn't seem to stop entire generations from emulating their behavior. Women have been portrayed as devious in everything from the Bible on up. I'm about as devious as a rabbit and so are most women on the spectrum, anyway. For the most part, we're too busy just trying to get along in the world, to make it a better place.

So you can see the conundrum. Accept the mantle of limitations placed upon your shoulder and all that it implies, or be banished from the kingdom. It's really a Hobson's choice. As much as I'd like to say the world is changing, it isn't changing fast enough for some of us.

Masculinity I believe males on the spectrum face similar conundrums. There are physical traits to autism that may not conform to male expectations from without. From within, I think there exists, regardless of testosterone, a similar dislike for gender stereotypes and expectations. Not taking to sports, not sharing any sense of masculine camaraderie or predispositions, may make males on the spectrum feel as isolated as we women do. Yet, as I mentioned above, while many men on the spectrum present as very gentle creatures, it is oft said that the autistic mind is a very male mind. So these gentle creatures can then surprise us with certain autistic traits that seem at odds with the rest of their personality, such as stubbornness, bluntness and meltdowns.

Both genders have to find their authenticity, decide if masculinity or femininity is important to them and redefine what it means. This will require not only trying on a lot of hats, but a few wardrobes as well. (See *Identity*.)

▶ **Gossip** Somehow along the way gossip turned into an acceptable form of entertainment. If it's harmless and superficial, that's one thing, but often gossip is the precursor to slander, persecution and even violence. What people say about others is sometimes how they feel about themselves. So if someone says kind things about others, they probably have a pretty healthy psyche. If, however, they are always spouting negativity about others, they are probably not very happy people. "That's all well and good" you may think, but if the slander is public and affecting your reputation, social standing and/or income, that's getting into troubling waters. In this case, official or legal protection might be called for. Sometimes gossip is just one person's opinion, e.g. "She's a nasty psychopath." But stating untrue events as facts, e.g. "She cheated on her husband," makes for fabrications that can have real, damaging, lasting consequences.

Social media has few protections. The playground has few protections. The office, too. The best thing to do is to not engage, to succinctly and clearly deny anything that must be denied, but not to get into a very murky battle of "he said/she said" that will lead down a seemingly endless path of aggravation and pain. Avoid name-calling at all costs. Just because someone called you a bitch is not license to return the favor. Take the high road, every time. Truth will out, eventually. It always does. Even when a government or nation wants to cover something up, eventually facts are revealed even if it takes decades or centuries. But in the lives of individuals, karma is usually much quicker. Be patient but be proactive, as opposed to reactive. Those who live to gossip usually become victims of their own poisonous, forked tongue.

▶ **Gratitude** The single most important ingredient for a happy and successful life is gratitude. Focusing on what is wrong or what is missing does not project the positive energy that will bring those things to us. Recognizing and having gratitude for what blessings we do have will open the door to more good things. This is not some silly platitude. This is the observation of a lifetime, my own and others', and seeing what works and what doesn't.

▶ **Grooming and hygiene** Shower, shave, moisturize, condition, pluck, wax, straighten, curl: it's an endless cycle of seemingly pointless attempts to stave off oils and aging. One is good for you and the other's inevitable so any sensible Aspie would ask, "What's the point?" Most so-called normal people, at least Americans, spend so much time on grooming you'd think there is a special brand of OCD reserved just for them. OCCD—obsessive cleanliness compulsion disorder.

Some amount of attention to these matters is necessary. Many of us are reclusive and practical, and will wander the dark halls of our abode with unkempt hair, five-day-old pajamas, and a green vapor emanating from our nether bits if we don't have to go out. What you look like is a reflection of your self-esteem and self-image. If you aren't clean, if you do get an urge or need to go somewhere, you won't be ready. If you look in a mirror, or someone drops by, you might be embarrassed. Bathe and groom regularly. You don't have to shower every day but at least every couple of days, and clean your clothes as well. Just because your girlfriend likes your odor doesn't mean your co-workers should be subjected to it. Natural is all well and good, but ladies, it's probably time to shave your legs when they require conditioner as opposed to moisturizer. I also suggest for anyone over the age of thirty to get a magnifying mirror. Our up-close vision goes as we get older and although we might not notice that our nose hairs are braiding, or we have more whiskers on our chin than Grandma Gert, and our eyebrows resemble curly fries with garlic sprinkles, a large portion of the public will.

▶ **Groups** I don't know how much our fear of groups is inherent in autism and how much is learned and acquired, but suffice to say the idea of walking into a classroom, club or other gathering can make us feel a little bit like a deer must entering a pen of hyenas. The fear part is likely acquired, but the reason we acquire it is partly because of what we exude. Early on, other kids will sense our difference, and our own propensity to self-isolate will combine to create a climate in which we stop being invited or first-picked, and we begin to view groups as unfriendly, unwelcoming things. This can extend to meetings at work, open-plan offices, social events and educational gatherings. The idea of entering an AS social group might be scary the first time, but we usually find, once we do, that the vibe is totally different and we won't get that same cold feeling running through our veins.

Your m.o. (modus operandi) can be the same in groups as in any social situation. Try to remember to breathe, relax your body posture, and turn your attention outward. Think not "I hope they like me and make me feel welcome," but "I will show them I am outgoing and will make them feel comfortable." This doesn't have to be manic or false: work it one person at a time, quietly, cautiously perhaps, rather than switching into entertainer mode as we sometimes do when that adrenalin kicks in.

Online groups can be much easier for us, but do be careful about joining them willy-nilly. Keyboard warriors abound, and online groups can have their own pecking order and bullying. It is certainly not all bad news though. Online groups can strengthen our social skills, and build a network of friends.

▶ **Gynecology visits** are an absolute necessity for women. Please see *Doctor visits*.

H

▶ **Happiness, joy and hope** I have found the key to happiness: it is a choice. This will anger some people, no doubt. Everyone, no matter what their circumstance, needs to find some joy in life. And while not advocating victim-blaming, even subjects of violent crimes or other unjust circumstances have control over how they deal with things and how they move on. There are people with every*thing* who are miserable, and others with no*thing* who are joyful. This proves happiness doesn't come from *things*.

At the end of the day, there is only your soul, your spirit, and it has to be a spirit of joyfulness, adding to the light of the world even if no one, and I mean no one, notices it.

Hope, like happiness and joy, comes from within, not without. The main difficulty most of us have is that we look for satisfaction and joy from external sources. Those are too fleeting, too transient. True happiness is a flame within you that you keep lit by effort and vigilance, not by neglect, despair and negative thinking. Do you ever notice that like attracts like? That's why good things often happen to those who don't need them as much as someone else might. Every time something good came to me, it wasn't when I was at my most down, it was when I had already managed to pick myself up when there seemed to be nothing to get up for.

Everyone will have their recipe for happiness, but there will be common factors among all who succeed. Hope, positive thinking and a capacity for joy. Not yachts, fame or beauty.

You will hit bumps in the road, but you will recover much quicker if you consciously decide to stay positive. It's like weight training for the mind. You will feel yourself getting stronger although sometimes you will get tired and want to quit. It's your choice: stay in Mirkwood with the spiders, or carry on to the light.

▶ **Health** (see *Diet*, *Body image*, *Vitality*)

▶ **Helpful** People on the spectrum generally like to feel useful and needed and one of the ways this is expressed is by being helpful to other people. We won't hesitate to open a door for the elderly, help a struggling co-worker with a task, or shovel out a neighbor's stuck car. One of the problems with this is we may expect others to be like us, and not understand it when we find others are not so forthcoming. Of course others may be helpful or generous in ways that are not so obvious to us, or they might be more guarded, and it isn't for us to judge them.

Another potential problem is that we may be easy to take advantage of. If you're always giving and not getting, it might be time to step back and get an overview of the situation. We can't all be Mother Theresas and martyrs. Balance in relationships, while not keeping score, is crucial so resentment doesn't build up. Watch out for being pedantic and too helpful when it isn't asked for.

▶ **Hermit** (see *Socializing*) I'm not a hermit, I'm elusive, reclusive and exclusive.

It seems that many of us lead hermit-like existences. Even though we may make constant forays into the world, I don't think there's an Aspie in the world who doesn't relish his or her alone time, having their favorite food, drink, entertainment, surrounded by their favorite pets or objects. If there is, I'd have to question their diagnosis.

It is so important for us to have homes that are conducive to sensory decompression, mood elevation and good health: much more so than non-autistics, who, as I've witnessed with my own eyes over the years, can live with a lot more noise and social stimuli than we can. It's not that they don't need their peace and quiet too, just not nearly as much of it.

Once again the question is balance. Tony Attwood has said we need one hour of down time for every hour of socializing, but I think we need an hour of socializing for every day of solitude. Whether that takes the form of a phone call or a visit, do reach out and get some every day.

I'm a hermit but I'm not dressed in white and sitting at a table with a moldy cake like Miss Havisham. I'm working, and reading, and writing, and playing, and laughing at films and wrestling with my dogs. I have a yoga and exercise room, a living room with a telly and a bay window, a spacious kitchen where I cook healthy meals for myself and sometimes friends, and an office/studio with a delightful view of animals and a far-off lake. Life is good if a little lonely at times. If the internet disappeared tomorrow, I'd have to update this report but at the moment, I'm peaceful. I think that what life lacks for so many of us on the spectrum is just peace, absence of stress, the feeling we are good enough as we are. Here in my little world, I'm good enough.

If you choose to be a hermit, or if the life chooses you, remember there's a big difference between stockpiling arms and stockpiling wisdom. Be sure you're in it for the right reasons.

▶ **Holidays** (see *Rest and relaxation*) If Aspies created holidays there would be Trekkie day, Tolkien day, Einstein day, invention of the microchip day, internet appreciation week. But given the ones we have, here are some pointers.

Aspies + expectations = anguish. Holidays carry a lot of weight and can bring out our best but also our worst memories and insecurities. They shine a light on the "flaws" in our lives, such as not having a partner or a lot of money. Strained family relationships tend to also be cast in the spotlight, but if family invites you, it's their way of reaching out and it could be a good gesture to accept. One caveat is the guilt call, the last-minute invitation from family. If someone invites you to Christmas dinner (or whatever), they should extend a proper invitation that doesn't make you feel devalued.

Even before the holidays, there's all this shopping pressure. Avoid crowds, rushes, inane music, etc. by shopping online, or better yet, visiting quiet, out-of-the-way shops that could really use your business. Local products like honey, jam, produce, baked goods, always have appeal and aren't very expensive. If you can't afford to buy, perhaps some homemade cookies or similar can be decorated and wrapped. If artistic, a nice homemade card can be made and copied on quality stock.

If you live alone and are not close to your family, people might not know you have nowhere to go on holidays. Seek and accept invitations. Or extend them to other loners like yourself.

It is said that people on the spectrum are great actors. At gatherings, don't be false, but putting forth the more positive, cheerful, fun side of yourself will make others feel comfortable around you, rather than sulking and playing up the black sheep role. Use your acting skills positively. Bring games or activities that you like, e.g. Trivial Pursuit, that you can play with a small number of people. Create an oasis in the chaos *and* have a script. Go all out and bring the script to *A Christmas Carol* and designate roles. (Well, *I'd* love that anyway.)

Bring your sensory toolkit: earplugs, squishy toys, hat with visor, and dress comfortably with layers, since crowded rooms can get very hot. Anything that comforts you should go into your purse or backpack.

Reading the paper or listening to music on headphones at gatherings is kind of rude and should be kept to a minimum or avoided altogether. This is a time to think about others as well as yourself. If you need cocoon time, perhaps find a quiet room to regroup or one person to have a good conversation with.

If you're worried about too much bad holiday music, bring something of your own to share. If you're a musician, play something. I once sang "Grandma got run over by a reindeer" to my gran and it was a memorable event.

Relying on others to feed us puts us in a vulnerable position. Bringing something to the table can really help, especially if you have special dietary needs. You can tell the host in advance that you'd like to bring one or two dishes of your own. You can ask if you should bring enough to share, since they may see that as usurping their chef role, or they may welcome the additional food. This is a much better way of handling the situation than eating food that isn't good for you, or going hungry and sulking because there's nothing you can safely eat. Rigidity can also make letting others cook for us difficult. Treat trying new foods as part of the fun of the holidays.

Be helpful and you will be guaranteed to feel welcome and useful. Do the dishes, clean up, put away discarded wads of wrapping paper. Be the one to take the dogs out. Play with the children. Fetch the firewood and stoke the fire. Shovel the path for arriving/departing guests.

Drinking to deal with family is never a good idea (see *Drinking to cope*). Alcohol is a depressant and will lower your control over your own emotions. If you have family issues, and unresolved anger or other problems, now is not a good time to air them. That is best handled sober, and most likely privately, between the concerned parties and not in front of all the children, friends and extended family members. Best to clear the air beforehand if possible. We tend to be on the shy side and might regret over-gregarious behavior afterward if we lose control because of too much "holiday cheer."

Alone because of geography or estrangement? Watching films all day can make the day seem long. Leave those for later. Do a project you've been putting off. Go for a walk, work out. Cook a nice meal with lots of courses for leftovers. Call or Skype with friends. Volunteer at a kitchen or nursing home. Have a musical skill? Perform at a hospice or nursing home. Start a book you've been meaning to read (or write). Put on old records and dance. Before Xmas, you can look into carol groups or church choirs. Also, face painting and other skills might be in demand at holiday fairs. Take a drive or walk to the country, a beach, park or local farm. Stay away from tourist traps. Treat your own pets to presents, pampering, dress-up and games. In winter, snowboard, ski, toboggan, sled. Feed the animals around you. Winter birds such as cardinals will flock to your home if you keep a feeder full all winter (so will deer, rabbits, voles and everything else, so be warned). Many northern cultures spend more winter time outside than we pampered Americans. Have a fire outdoors and enjoy it. Bundle up and have a nice cup of tea! Build a snowman (or igloo if you live where I do!).

It's just one day. If you haven't had a good one, make plans for the next holiday to avoid the same old blues. Create your own holiday reality. If that means being alone, so be it. But remember, if others need you, and love you, you don't want to disregard their feelings. But nor should you throw your love at those who don't want it. Find your true family!

▶ **Honesty** (see *Bluntness*) Bluntness and brutal honesty tend to be a trait of the autism spectrum. If you don't want an honest opinion on your new hairstyle, best not to ask us. Of course, this is a generalization, and plenty of us have learned the art of tact and diplomacy. I almost think that this is one way to tell a person on the spectrum from people with conditions that share traits with the autism spectrum. I've met those who claim to be Asperger's but seem dishonest, if not compulsive liars, who may not have been properly assessed. Perhaps they have just taken acting too far and have not yet found the value of authenticity.

While we have as hard a time as anyone hearing the cold truth, we prefer it over dishonesty. Never lie to an Aspie, or we will find it very difficult to trust you again. We may forget and let it happen over and over, but eventually we will put your picture on our mental wall like a most wanted poster, except it will read "least wanted."

As a rule, we do not lie, but for many Aspies there is a notable exception: to institutions upholding rules we deem unfair. For example, you might think the car inspection (MOT for Brits) is an unnecessary expense and put your Aspie ingenuity to work in creating a false sticker for your windshield. This, to us, isn't lying, it is more like playing chess. A person on the spectrum who is engaged in this sort of behavior needs to learn that there are consequences for breaking rules, even ones we deem ridiculous. After all, none of us has perfect judgment and we may be biased or rationalizing. We may be breaking the law and in danger of legal and penal retribution.

As for delivering truth, learning to frame your words so that you get your point across but don't lose a friend in the process can be a subject of special interest and a very rewarding one at that. Words shot like arrows may be the most expedient, but they can prove lethal to budding friendships.

▶ **Humiliation** (and avoiding it or getting past it) People with Asperger's can be easy to make fun of since we don't usually realize when it's happening, or if we do, we become frozen with mortification and can't speak. Our brains can become thick and foggy and our tongues tied (see *Selective mutism*).

From early childhood we won't act as expected and very often become "figures of fun," bearing the brunt of jokes. There's a fine line between healthy rib-poking and cruel humiliation (see *Bullying*) and as you get older you will be able to discern the difference more easily. Children and even grown-ups will often test each other with humor, to see what the other is made of; i.e., if they're someone they can have fun with, or if they are humorless and touchy. Of course there are also jackasses who just want to be cruel. You can learn to tell over time. The latter type still shocks me, but I finally realize they do exist, unfortunately.

Having a sense of humility and humor will help you through these moments. Meaning, everyone should be humble enough to laugh at themselves from time to time, and also, it's okay to try and give as good as you get. A clever comeback isn't always forthcoming, but with practice, can get easier.

Try not to carry a chip on your shoulder from these events, or expect them to keep occurring. The mind is adaptive and learns and grows. You can try and catch things as they happen and say something right then and there, even if it means risking embarrassment. As long as you don't lose your temper you'll still have your dignity. Learn to stand up for yourself. If, for example, a customer service rep (strangely some of the rudest people on the planet) insults you, you can respond with, "If you prefer customers you can insult I'd better take my money elsewhere." It will make them think for a moment, and you won't have blown your top and gotten thrown out. This kind of in-the-moment response helps avert the regret of both missing an opportunity to self-advocate and melting down in public.

▶ **Humility and humor** These are tools you may never find in any Asperger's self-help manuals because there's so much emphasis on pride. Humility is not an antonym of pride, no matter what Webster's says. It's an antidote to too much. It's the ability to say "Nobody's perfect, not even me, and that's okay." I group this with humor, because it's another antidote to too much pride, or to embarrassment and humiliation. If you can laugh at yourself, not in chronic self-deprecation but on occasion, as needed, it makes you less likely to be made fun of by others in a potentially painful situation.

▶ **Hyperlexia** is sometimes called "little professor syndrome." It is the autodidactic ability to read beyond one's chronological years. Many boys and girls on the spectrum display this tendency. I was one such child and I recall completely and clearly my motivations, of which there were two. First, I loved stories and could not stand to wait for bedtime or for my mother to take a break from housekeeping to read to me. At age three, I asked her to read the *A is for Apple* alphabet book one more time, paying careful attention to the sound of each letter, and I was off, reading books on my own from that day forward. Second, I was obsessed with the film *To Sir With Love*, which I had seen once. I wanted to know when it was going to be on again. The only way to know was to read the movie section of the weekly TV newspaper which came every Sunday. No one would read it for me. I can remember skimming the TV guide every week and the tremendous satisfaction when, months later, I found the entry, and sure enough, was able to watch the film that very week.

Hyperlexia is a form of giftedness, and is one of many reasons that little children may have their autism overlooked. We may give the impression of maturity at a very young age, but later, especially when puberty hits, our emotional and social deficits become more noticeable.

▶ **Hypersensitivity** (or being thin-skinned) (see *Sensory issues*) Not long ago, it was thought people on the spectrum felt less than others, but Markram and Markram's theory of autism[25] postulated that those with autism were *hyper*sensitive, not *hypo*, and most works since reflect that. Many people do have high pain thresholds but most of us have sensitivities at least in some areas, such as to noise, lights, smells, etc. Many of us even have painful skin when we are children, which is why we are so fussy about what we wear. As we get older, some of this may dissipate, and some things may worsen, especially if we have shattered nerves from PTSD or other reasons.

We can also be sensitive to criticism. The Buddhists say, "The mind is an untrained monkey," and I do so love this analogy. I'm also reminded of the tarot card Strength, which is about subduing some of our animal nature, gaining control over our passions and senses. Being sensitive is good—without sensitive people we'd have no poets and artists. Being hypersensitive is a pain not just to you but sometimes also those around you. It is something you can learn to control by applying much of the advice in this book: diet, exercise, humility and humor, sensory tools, it's all here.

I

▶ **Identity** Because we feel like actors on a stage without any script, people on the spectrum learn by mimicking others. But we don't intrinsically understand what we're mimicking. We often feel like blank pieces of paper that need to be filled with experiences in order to create our identity. Other kids just seem like they're born with a script, a role, an identity.

As a result it takes a while for this journey, and we may try on many different personalities along the way, even changing countries, accents, gender identity. This can give the impression of someone who is flighty and insincere, a faker, when really it's an earnest quest to find oneself.

Relax. You are a character already, even if you don't feel like you are anything special. After a lifetime of exploration, you may find you come full circle back to where you were as a child (if you ever left). Same interests, same morals, but with an air of maturity and confidence born of experience. This tendency to seek, explore and create ourselves is what makes us interesting and compassionate people.

▶ **Imagination** (see *Creativity, Escapism, Talent*) It was long thought that people on the spectrum were not imaginative. Perhaps that had to do with the "lack of social imagination" criteria in some diagnostic manuals. It is true we have a harder time with that and with theory of mind, but imagination we may have in spades. Writers, composers, artists, inventors, these occupations and more are swelled with countless ranks of spectrumites. Many of us spend our days, especially as children, imagining a more peaceful, inclusive world, and our adulthoods trying to create that.

▶ **Immunization** I have never publicly weighed in on the immunization–autism debate. There are several studies that show there is no link, but scientific studies can be slanted at worst, and are not foolproof at best. There is plenty of anecdotal evidence (and as we know, the plural of anecdote is *data*) to suggest that the combined MMR vaccine may have impacted the onset of autism in children.

When it comes to your children you have to make as informed and weighed an opinion as you can. I would suggest reading, researching, going on forums, and then looking at the pros vs. the cons. Some parents have requested three separate shots, to give their children time to assimilate one live viral vaccine at a time, but at the time of this writing, there are no longer separate vaccines available as an option in the United States.

▶ **i-muscles** (see *Bullying, Social media, Trolls*) The virtual equivalent of beer muscles, flexed and wielded by *keyboard warriors*. Rude behavior online which masquerades as courage but is instead plain old cowardice.

▶ **Independence** (see *Sexism*) As a person on the spectrum, you will not have the same camaraderie with your fellow human that a non-autistic will. As you go through life, there may be episodes of eating lunch alone, spending weekends alone, working alone, that sort of thing. Some will work hard to create support networks and friendships, but chances are that as a result of this lone wolfiness, you may find you are more independent than most people you know.

If something breaks in my house and needs repairs, I generally have two choices: fix it myself, or hire some inevitably NA guy with his ass hanging out of his pants who will see that I've no one to protect me from his random price-hikes. (Now, if only he'd hike up those pants.) I recently hired a plumber who laughed when I asked a perfectly reasonable layperson's question about my boiler. I responded, "Let's make a deal. You don't laugh at me for not knowing plumbing and I won't laugh at you for not being able to compose music or write books." I'd like to say that fixed the situation, but instead he left and never came back.

Thanks to adult education and YouTube, other than a surgical procedure there are very few things I can't sort out myself. The danger? Feeling like a know-it-all and not asking for help when you really do need it. There's fun and joy in collaboration, though it is good to be as self-sufficient as possible.

Avoid the *disability armchair,* the place you fall into where you atrophy and don't expand your abilities. I know people who are in their thirties who've never been away from home although they really don't seem very affected, but they've never challenged themselves. Being independent at least in some areas will bolster your self-esteem and courage, and give you the appetite for even more skills to add to your list.

Financial independence is also important, even more so here in the US as opposed to other countries. There are safety nets here, but you have to fall and hit the ground first before they'll pull them out. Banking on a spouse or partner to support you is dangerous too—it puts pressure on that relationship on top of what's already going to be there. When I talk to someone on the spectrum who gives me a long list of what they can't do as opposed to what they can, I see that some reprogramming is needed. Anyone can make at least a little bit of money, doing *something*, whether it's babysitting, baking, dogwalking, selling home-grown veggies, etc.

▶ **Insomnia** (see *Rest and relaxation, Sleep issues*)

▶ **Instincts and intuition** People on the spectrum, if they're healthy mentally, can have finely tuned instincts and intuition. Partly because we spend so much time alone with our thoughts, we learn to hear our own inner voice louder than some, but we may also learn to doubt ourselves.

Social instincts My friend Sara said it perfectly:

> When someone is used to missing basic social cues, it's easy to fall into the trap of believing you miss *all* cues. In fact, I think Aspies are extremely insightful but in a completely different way from neurotypicals. If an Aspie picks up on something instinctually but looks for reassurance from a neurotypical, quite often that neurotypical won't see the same thing. Being socially wrong so often, the Aspie is inclined to think they must be the one who is misreading the person or situation. Oftentimes, the Aspie is proved right much later. Because Aspies tend to be somewhat socially blind, they have the ability to see past the social exterior of a person and don't feel the burden of accepting someone's veneer.

So perhaps it's not so much the conclusions we draw about people that are erroneous, but the fact that we don't trust those conclusions until it's too late.

I think many neuroses and compulsions may be the result of not trusting your intuition—a prime example would be the person who goes back to check that they turned the stove off. They will invariably say that they are sure they did, but then add that they're not sure. By not trusting our instincts, which all animals have, we learn self-doubt, insecurity.

If we don't trust our own instincts, we may let people into our lives that we shouldn't. We need to follow others' advice in certain situations, such as dating safely, until we have a track record of proven good instincts. Anyhow, it never hurts to get a second opinion.

Everyone is different; perhaps your own instincts are buried, you've become detached and you need to cultivate them through quiet meditation, practice and life experience. Learn to trust your intuition and every tiny event becomes like a gentle push keeping you on your path. It doesn't matter if you believe this is external, from a higher power, or internal from your own source; it works.

It's good to listen to your inner voice; however, if you have inner voic*es*, that's a different thing entirely, especially if they argue with one another or tell you to do bad things.

▶ **Intelligence** In my other books, I wrote that people on the spectrum have a *higher fluid intelligence* than non-autistics…in very simple terms, this is the ability to teach yourself what you want to learn, to come up with new ways of doing things, or just knowing things that you couldn't possibly know, for example how to play the piano the first time you ever sit down at one.

When I was a little girl, there was one thing I had the utmost confidence in and that was my own intelligence. I knew I didn't know everything, and that frustrated me, so I read voraciously, craved adventures and experiences, so I could add knowledge to that intelligence. When you go out into a world that tells you that you are wrong about so many things, and you know you aren't, it is very frustrating. You learn to doubt yourself or to doubt others, or both at alternating times (see *Instincts and intuition*).

What the truth has turned out to be is this: yes, I am smart. However, that doesn't mean I am always right. No one is. That is probably the hardest lesson for us Aspies to learn. When we are wrong about something, it doesn't mean that we are intrinsically wrong (see *Black and white thinking*). The trick is to travel full circle back to where you were when you were little and had confidence in your own mind, only now you are carrying a backpack of knowledge, humility and hopefully some respect for the knowledge of others (see *Know-it-all*).

There are people who will tell you you're wrong simply because you are incorrect about something. There are those who will tell you you're wrong because they're mean, ignorant or just mistaken. Learning to tell the difference is the part where self-confidence and humility come into play.

▶ **Introspection** (see *Self-centered and selfish*) Socrates said, "The unexamined life is not worth living." As a professional hermit, my life is not only examined, it's dissected and laid out on a table under glaring light. This is also part of the reason we make good writers and speakers; we understand human nature by making ourselves a special course of study.

It is difficult to turn your attention outward, if you feel you don't have a tribe, if you are having difficulty getting your basic needs met, or if your self-esteem is low. Eventually, however, as we work on those things, we can raise our gaze from our navel to our neighbor. There's more to life than self-awareness—there's using it for the good of others.

▶ **IRL** An abbreviation of *in real life*, as opposed to URL, which means *uniform resource locator*, but could easily stand for *unreal life*.

▶ **Irlen lenses** These are person-specific colored lenses worn as glasses or contacts, designed to aid in the correction of *scotopic sensitivity syndrome*, or *Irlen syndrome*. These are said to be visual/perception problems related to light (source, glare, luminance, wavelength) and black/white contrast. These difficulties lead to reading problems, eye strain, headaches, migraines and other physical difficulties.

According to Irlen, the syndrome has six characteristics:

1. photophobia (abnormal intolerance to visual perception of light)

2. eye strain

3. poor visual resolution

4. a reduced span of focus

5. impaired depth perception

6. poor sustained focus.

Clients are diagnosed via interview and observation while performing visual tasks such as reading and geometric identification. This is yet another case of science vs. anecdote. People on the spectrum whom I've met who wear the lenses, swear by them. One fellow I met in Scotland said he never really saw his wife's face in one cohesive image until he had Irlen lenses. Yet, if you look, there are plenty of articles that claim research shows no significant improvement of reading and other visual-related tasks. I'd suggest if you have visual impairments that traditional methods do not improve, it might be worth seeking an Irlen specialist and seeing if they can help you.

J

▶ **Joint attention** is the shared attention of two individuals on an object initiated by gaze or pointing. It tends to be impaired in classic autism, less so as a person moves further along the autism spectrum towards the high-functioning end. Perhaps this joint attention deficit in Asperger's manifests as preference for solitary activities such as reading, spending time on devices, and enjoying activities alone that others may prefer to do with people, such as watching films.

This, in my humble opinion, stems from our ability to sense others in a different way, getting so many unspoken signals that we are overwhelmed and distracted. For example, I have a sister with whom I find it extremely difficult to watch films, as she "thinks too loud." In fact, I find most if not all people a distraction when watching something. I prefer to do things that require any focus alone. Whether this is connected to a joint attention deficit is unknown, but since this is a common preference in Asperger's, I think it's worth exploring. I may be full of beans but sometime they turn out to be magic beans.

▶ **Joking** (see *Humility and humor, Humiliation*) I once had lunch with a well-known writer, speaker and Aspie, a very affable fellow with a great sense of humor. At the table he would repeatedly make humorous comments, but his jokes kept going over my head. And mine went over his head. It was like a bad game of tennis, where both players could serve but neither return.

Learning to make jokes is an important social skill to cultivate but it's only Phase One; learning to catch when someone else is joking is Phase Two of the operation. Phase Three is learning to take a joke. Being made fun of happens to us perhaps too often: so much so that watching *The Office* and other cringe-inducing comedies may be anything but entertaining to you. Every once in a while we need to be able to laugh at ourselves. Getting pink ears and having a meltdown is only going to add to the cycle of pain.

Sometimes when people pick on you it isn't meant to be mean, it's meant to say that you are a part of their club. Even if this seems Neanderthal to you, most of us do it when we get really comfortable with someone. Personally I can't abide being with people who can't take a tiny bit of ribbing. Life gets a whole lot easier once we learn to take some. If it's truly mean-spirited, turn it around or walk away. Learning to tell the difference takes time. You can ask, "What did you mean by that?" or ask a trusted friend if the person was being mean-spirited. Once you get some practice you can learn to give as good as you get; just don't go overboard. It takes us a while to learn the steps of this dance. Watching comics and comedies is a great way to start. Studying humor will teach us its myriad subtle—and not so subtle—ways.

Tip: if someone makes a joke on social media, don't type "I don't get this." If something doesn't make you laugh, why bring attention to yourself? The very first comment on the very first comedy video I posted on Facebook was "Don't quit your day job" by an Aspie friend with no joke-ometer. I took the video down, but then reposted it later that day. Every other comment was positive and it even got shared on *Wired Magazine* by a respected journalist. Being the sour dour puss is something we all do, but we shouldn't thrust it on those who are seeking a few laughs in this life.

I once made a joke and a man chided, "Puns are the lowest form of humor." I wish I'd responded with "Low humor is better than no humor." He was what scientists refer to as a "pompous twit."

▶ **Journaling** (see *Writing*)

▶ **Judgmental** We have all been judged. We are all judgmental. It's a pretty exhausting occupation. In this case, I'm siding with the Bible. Let he who has not sinned cast the first stone. Of course, sometimes we need to intervene— someone who is wreaking harm or havoc should be stopped and restrained, but so much judgmentalism in our lives is of the petty, gossipy variety. Giving it a rest, being less critical, makes us nicer to be around and less likely to be the recipient of judgment.

K

▶ **Know-it-all** (see *Pedantry*) I held an informal survey online: "You know you're an Aspie when…" and someone answered, "…you're the smartest one in the room." Ouch. A truly smart individual would never say such a thing. It is incredibly repelling to others and alienating to the utterer. Since this person was on social media, one could safely assume they'd like to have friends.

No one is suggesting you dumb yourself down. Not in the slightest, but as a consultant for people on the spectrum the biggest challenge I have is working with the know-it-all. For a few reasons: first, because I'm probably one of those and no one dislikes know-it-alls as much as another know-it-all. Probably the biggest hurdle my clients face is realizing that they are not infallibly correct. Black and white thinking can make it difficult for some of us to admit mistakes. It is incredibly limiting intellectually and socially to think you possess the perfect insight into every situation.

We've all known (or been) that kid in class who shoots his or her hand up first like lightning at every question the teacher asks. If this were sports, where competitiveness is praised, perhaps that person would be admired. But most sports require teamwork. In the classroom, allowing others to take the ball now and then, and quietly being pleased with your intellectual prowess, may be a good exercise in strength and humility.

If you were truly omnipotent and omniscient, you wouldn't be reading this book. The same desire to learn from books can guide your social conversations. Take an interest in what others are saying, and try not to cut them off before they finish their sentences. Cultivate the fine art of listening.

▶ **Knowledge** (see *Intelligence*) There's prejudice against knowledge in a lot of cultures, including religious culture, even, and I'm nervous to say it, Christianity. I'm sorry but if someone puts me in a garden and says "Don't eat the fruit of knowledge," I'm eating it. Knowledge is what makes humans different from animals. They have instincts, strong survival instincts, but we have knowledge. Knowledge can be erroneous, misleading, incorrect, trendy, but it can also be enlightening, creative, life-saving, mind-blowing, planet-improving, etc.

It is tempting for some of us to think we know it all, but critical thinking, seeking and applying knowledge and evidence, with logic, rational thinking and open-mindedness (and a splash of creative intuition), separates the truly intelligent from the stagnant.

L

▶ **Labels** (see *Diagnosis, Asperger's: As a label*) What good is a label? If it weren't for labels, we wouldn't be able to say "Pass the spoon," we'd have to say, "Pass that round thing with the long thing to hang onto." They're a necessary thing that of course has the inherent danger of limiting how others think of us. They give us a frame of reference for understand our own behavior and why we seem to be different than the majority. In the beginning of this process, labels are necessary for bringing into focus differences and disparities. If it weren't for loud men and women spouting labels, we would not have equal rights for any minorities. Once things become more equal, then labels become much less necessary. There's no point in pointing out differences and making things equal, if we then don't acknowledge and appreciate our similarities.

In the case of the rights of women, ethnic minorities or physically disabled people, it's more obvious who they are, but in the case of higher functioning ASCs (autism spectrum conditions), our struggles are less apparent so our situation is more unique and perhaps more difficult to get acknowledgement and redress. When we are first diagnosed, we may want to change the world. With the label comes explanation, but that explanation will not be easy to share with the world; to make it listen. The label in our case is more for our own benefit, our internal process, than to make significant changes in the world around us.

To define is also to limit. You are more than a label, so don't let others' perceptions limit you. You are what you think you are to a large extent.

▶ **Listening** (or pain and trauma vs. the art of being PRESENT) Recently I conducted an experiment on social media. I made a post that essentially said that while some obesity has legitimate cause, most of it is due to bad choices and lack of exercise. What a kerfuffle ensued! Within minutes, I was accused of bigotry, hatred, and saying, "All fat people should die." I was accused of saying everyone should be skinny and that they should starve themselves, none of which was true. (The most vitriolic reactions seemed to be from people who were still engaging in unhealthy eating habits and were defensive of them. Those who said they had weight issues but were working on eating healthily were not at all combative.) I repeatedly asked people to clear their minds, and read my words calmly, but they only went farther and farther down the road of making me feel like Hitler incarnate for pointing out what is pretty obvious, at least here in America.

We all have emotional reactions to others' words that may color what we hear. Memories of experiences and sensations lodge in our minds and bodies, they never leave us entirely, so that when something sparks that memory, it might evoke a reaction that is well beyond what the current situation calls for. When you have a life filled with trauma and pain, as so many autistics and Aspies do, you can develop a real chip on your shoulder which will prevent you from seeing clearly in the present and future, and may prevent you from living life fully and with all possible enjoyment. Add to that our already hypersensitive nature and you can see how we'd be touchy if not testy at times. Mindfulness is the answer: meditation is one method of achieving it, or yoga, or undergoing years of talk therapy. Through these things you can learn to really listen to what someone is saying…then try not to knee jerk every time you *think* someone's being a jerk.

Sometimes, it's not so much a case of we hear what we *want* to hear, as it is we hear what we *don't* want to hear.

▶ **Literal thinking** is one aspect of being on the autism spectrum I could have lived without. Part of the reason for literal thinking is that we have to concentrate so hard on what other people are saying in order to understand them that there is little room to look for subtext. For those of you not on the spectrum, it's kind of like asking someone for directions on a busy city street corner next to a construction site with a jackhammer going and heavy traffic whizzing by, with horns blaring and high winds blowing everyone about. You'd have to focus very hard to block out extraneous information. You wouldn't think that literal thinking has anything to do with diet and exercise and sensory tools and social skills training but these things are all linked. If we practice talking with others, if we have our sensory toolkit, if we are healthy, then we will be more relaxed in social situations and more likely to get the jokes. Why do you think we love films? We can be relaxed while we watch them, and can catch the jokes and idioms like Yogi Berra caught baseballs.

On the plus side this trait forces us to be good listeners. We also may be very good at communicating our thoughts, since we know what we want from others, and many of us become writers and public speakers. On the down side, we take people at their word when perhaps we shouldn't. A few bumps on the road are inevitable. Your family and friends should help look out for you, not make fun of you when you get this wrong.

▶ **Love** Lust makes us do silly things for a moment. Love makes us do silly things for a lifetime. See *Relationships*, *Dating*, *Sex* for practical advice.

▶ **Luck, karma and success** I recently saw a news story about an experiment in which scientists rigged a game of Monopoly. The winners felt entitled to win, even looking down on the losers. This says a lot about human nature. I think that when people are happy, they tend to blame those who are sad for bringing it on themselves, and are arrogant in their own happiness, feeling they deserve it while the sad ones don't. The trick to not burning out your good fortune is to appreciate it and share it and not blame those who are down on their luck, whatever the reason.

Live long enough and you really begin to see the workings of karma. We're all slaves to the law and that's what these young players don't realize. Break a heart or break someone's leg—it will come back to you. I've seen instant karma and

I've seen slow karma, but it always comes around. *That* is what they should teach in schools. It's the only religious doctrine anybody really needs.

The old saying is "Luck is opportunity meets preparedness." Every time I got lucky, it was after I made myself ready to meet it, and greet it dead in the eye. If luck comes knocking on your door, you won't be able to answer it if you're curled up in bed in a fetal position. Even when you've no obvious reason to get up, you never know what might be coming. (See *Happiness, joy and hope*, *Depression*.)

▶ **Machines** How we love our machines, from computers to cars, trains to rockets, gadgets, gizmos of all sorts. They possess no emotion, nor do they require any from us. Some people on the spectrum have developed emotional attachments to machines which they have personified, from cars to refrigerators. They will get no judgment here. Whatever makes you happy.

Many of us will become engineers and inventors, finding blissful satisfaction in the creation of machines that will elevate mankind in large and small ways, and will feed off the never-ending quest to improve and perfect the next one. This can be a wonderful life for us. Of course, your human nature will also most likely whisper in your ear to seek out human companionship of one sort or another, so don't forget to develop your social skills to some degree.

▶ **Manifesting** (aka magic, wish fulfillment and the power of the mind) When we are children we read stories about magic and believe them. Then as we grow up, that belief is diluted and negated by common sense. But as we get older to the point where we have seen and done so much, we come to realize that magic, the power to manifest things, does exist. It takes a bit longer than waving a magic wand, but nevertheless our thoughts do create a kind of worm hole whereby we teleport ourselves to where we need to be, or teleport to us the things we need to have.

How much we create for ourselves with our thoughts and actions and how much is destiny or fate (or god) will vary from person to person. You may disagree that destiny exists. That's fine. The part that matters here is free will and positive thought. Thinking about what you don't want may bring that very thing about. Try focusing your thoughts on what you do want. It's not seeing is believing; it's believing is seeing.

▶ **Manners** I'm beginning to think that manners are considered a sign of weakness. It is not weakness to say *excuse me*, or *I'm sorry* or to call someone to say *I'll be late*. Manners are the oil that makes society run smoothly. There are too many common transgressions to list them all, but my two current peeves are those who spend time on their smartphones when in the company of others, and people who monologue and don't care how others think or feel. In this *Me* generation, it can be preoccupying to seem stylish and cool. Sometimes just being polite (though not overly so) is all you need to do to make others comfortable around you. (See *Consideration for others*.)

▶ **Masturbation** (see *Sex*) Everyone, or nearly everyone, does it or has done it. It's part of sexual exploration, and, despite what you may have been told, is a normal and healthy thing to do. It teaches you about your body, what feels good, what doesn't, how to climax, etc. It only becomes a problem if it is done too frequently and in inappropriate places, and in lieu of developing relationships with others.

Masturbation can become a soothing behavior (stim) for some of us. That's all well and good, but one must be sure to have absolute privacy before engaging. If you are in public but hiding behind something, that is not good—one can be arrested for such behaviors. If you share a room with others, even if you think they are asleep, they may not be. You do not want to inflict this act upon others. They may find it upsetting and you will acquire an unwanted reputation.

Because of sensory issues, some might not have a lot of feeling down there and need to be careful they do not injure themselves trying to get satisfaction. Others have a lot of feeling in their genitals and will find it hurts to touch. You may have to seek out very specific information (through sex therapy, books, etc.) and experiment to find a way to have sexual activity in your life that doesn't hurt.

For some, it is so pleasurable they cannot get enough. We need to watch for obsessive, OCD-like masturbation. Although it's tempting to say, "At least when I masturbate, I'm having sex with someone I love," connecting with others is part of our jobs as human beings.

▶ **Math** I think that the reason some autistics like math so much is its lack of subjectivity. There tends to be one right answer to a problem. Other subjects in school tend to be graded on things like essay writing, and grading can be arbitrary. But in math, you are either right or wrong. Sometimes methodology is graded and if we solve a problem using our own method as opposed to the one we're told to, we may lose points and this will infuriate us. But apart from that, its simplicity is beautifully freeing. It's kind of like being on a train, another autism favorite. There's one track, no choices, no random turns to make. Simple and beautiful.

Some of us aren't good at math. So what? I refuse to use words like *dyscalculia*. We all have our strengths and weaknesses. Work with your strengths, work on your deficits, but don't medicalize every challenge you have.

▶ **Maturity** Aspies are often called little professors when they are young because of hyperlexia and a forthright manner. Many of us are seen as gifted children, mature and wise beyond our years. What is not so apparent is that we don't mature in the same way as non-autistic children. Physically, we may not develop as early (although some of us do, and that creates its own set of problems) as our peers. Emotionally, we tend to hold on to the same interests we had as children, throughout puberty, and indeed, some of us will hang on to the same interests throughout our lives, whether it's Star Wars, Harry Potter, astronomy, or whatever. This is fantastic, but it can create problems for us at puberty when girls are expected to start wearing the mantle of flirt, nurturer, social creature, shopper, makeup wearer and all that other stuff. Society really hasn't moved on. Boys are expected to be ball-playing, stoic, macho, girl-chasers, etc. (see *Gender issues*). Of course, different schools, different subcultures, will not have these same rigid expectations but by and large they do exist and have created lots of little neuroses and problems for millions of us black sheep.

Add to that the sensory and social issues that make us vacillate between shy quiet creatures, motor-mouths and meltdown-ers, and we may remain, in many ways, anomalistic mysteries. Truth is, we are in many ways children a lot longer than non-autistics. While steps must be taken to acquire some savvy to the ways of the world, one of the most beautiful gifts of the autistic is this child-like quality. It must be treasured and protected. We can't mature and become your version of a grown-up because you'd like us to. We are our own species in that regard.

▶ **Medication** Many of you may be living happily or at least better, with the help of modern chemistry. For others, medication will be the last resort in our search for a better life. As an adult it is your choice. But remember, as of this writing, there is no pill to cure autism!

Someone once told me their child's teacher asked if there was a pill the child could take to make them easier to deal with. I suggested they ask if there was any pill the teacher could take to make it easier to deal with their child! Such a request is heinous. I am not a teacher but what kind of unenlightened fool asks a parent to give an eight-year-old mind-altering substances?

I am also not a doctor. This is not a medical book so don't sue me for saying this, but Jesus God in heaven what is with all the pharmaceuticals? *Prilosec*? How about changing your diet? *Prozac*? How about doing something that challenges you and gets you out of your head for a day? *Viagra*? Why do you think golf was invented? To give old geezers something to do. There is no common sense ruling the airwaves, only Big Pharma. I went to the emergency room for the first time in years and they wanted to give me antibiotics without waiting to see if I had an illness that warranted it first!

I do get upset that millions and billions of children are being made to think that nature did not provide them with the foods and the remedies for almost all of what will ever ail them.

There are plenty of holistic remedies, many of which are known to work. People who take Echinacea tincture rarely get colds or flu. And common sense dictates that active people who eat a lot of fresh, organic, natural food will likely have fewer health problems than a lazy fast-food lover. But things can and do go wrong in the healthiest body and in addition to western medicine, it doesn't hurt to hit a variety of alternative sources, from books to the internet to your local alternative medicine practitioner, to find out what natural things have been known to help. You won't get any FDA (Food and Drug Administration) approvals on most of these things. Big Pharma holds all the cards in today's society. But if a lot of people say something works, it probably does.

If you are taking meds be warned that some holistic remedies can counteract their efficacy and vice versa. Do a little enquiring before mixing and matching anything. You can call your local pharmacist as they will have access to a database, but be sure to tell them *exactly* what you are taking, e.g. tincture as opposed to capsule, etc.

There are many different forms of alternative medicine, from acupuncture to *Zang Fu* Chinese medicine. Some of them have been around for thousands of years. However, sometimes western medicine is the way to go. Read, research, ask around, decide for yourself, and stay as informed as possible. Get all records from your doctor visits and read them for yourself to see if you are progressing as you should be.

Side effects If you think of all the substances in the last century that had FDA approval and then turned out to have horribly dangerous side effects, you won't be so trusting every time a soft-spoken lady comes on the TV and tells you that all you need is a little pill and your life will be all better. When it comes to pharmaceuticals, there's no free lunch. It seems that everything you take will have some side effect, from minor to serious: obesity, liver or kidney damage, drowsiness, seizures, birth defect, colored urine, stomach upsets and a million other things that might be worse than the symptom for which they are prescribed. I once saw "leaking anus" as a side effect of a pill that was created to make people not gain weight from eating. What?!? No wonder people lost weight— I'd think twice about a slice if I thought it was going to come squirting out of my butt on the way home from a date. Kind of makes me wonder where exactly we are on the evolutionary scale. You've heard the commercials: a soft-focus lens on some flowers, a comforting woman's voice tells you about some medicine that will help you out of depression, and then at the end this gnome from hell rattles off a list of possible side effects at warp speed.

When it comes to your mental and physical health, no one values your safety and well-being more than you do, except maybe your mother. When it comes to pharmaceuticals, trust no one source implicitly. I mean it. Even if you love your doctor or psychiatrist, they are given medications to give people. According to the website Consumer Reports, a half million doctors in the US had ties to Big Pharma and according to Propublica, in 2013 they paid at least $4 billion in some way to doctors, hospitals, clinics, teaching institutions, etc., and that is from a study in which only 50 percent of the existent US companies reported.[26] This is a distinct conflict of interest. Rich pharmaceutical companies can push their experimental drugs through, while a proven holistic remedy like Echinacea, made from regular old coneflowers that many of us have in our gardens, can't legally claim to prevent colds even though millions of people use it, swear by it and know that it does. While holistic remedies can cancel out or affect pharmaceuticals, and you should always check to see if there are interactions, generally they are far more benign than their modern laboratory replacements.

▶ **Meditation** can be physical, like breathing meditation or walking meditation, or simply be words you utter aloud or in your mind. It can be a prayer, like a Christian prayer, or a Buddhist mantra. It can be short and easy like *Nam Myoho Renge Kyo*, or long and complex, full of hidden power and meaning. It can even simply be a statement of gratitude, such as "Thank you for all the blessings in my life." Prayers that *ask* for something are not usually considered meditation, although there are meditations for empowerment.

Regardless of your spiritual persuasions, meditating is a good way to stop, connect, be mindful, be grateful and stop worrying for a few moments. To worry on a problem denotes stress and anxiety, things not conducive to good planning and decision-making. To meditate on something facilitates clear, calm, rational thought, and that can't be bad.

Meditation helps with mindfulness and with manifesting positive events and outcomes by harnessing good energies, whether from within or without.

▶ **Meltdowns** are like tsunamis. If you encounter an Aspie having one, run, grab a tree, and hang on for dear life. Don't try to reason with the meltdown, restrain it, or do anything; you are powerless until it passes. The instinct of the well-intentioned non-autistic might be to try and hug us or hold us tight in the middle of a nuclear meltdown, but you have to stand back and let it pass. You might think or say things like, "You need to be able accept comfort when you are hurting," and you'd be right, except you're not; meltdowns are the exception to that rule. Just stay back, do not engage, and try to keep yourself—and us—safe. We'll be back with you in a little while.

We have meltdowns because of sensory overload, extreme emotional upset, gross injustice or whatever spark just lit the fuse. Know that it takes a while for this sort of pressure to build up. Even if it appears to be triggered by something slight, there's probably a lot of anxiety and other stuff that's been building up pressure inside. During a meltdown, we may say and do things we later regret but you can bet there will be elements of repressed truth and suppressed anger that become shrapnel that can hit you and anyone else around.

If you have meltdowns, know that it is not a life sentence. If you follow the advice in this book on health, meditation, relationships, social skills, sensory issues, etc. you will see a significant drop in episodes, because you will have less anxiety, your nerves will be stronger and you will have less aggravation from external sources. Meltdowns can cost you relationships, jobs, custody of children, and get you thrown out of stores you may need in the future. They are damaging to everyone, but especially you. Of course they may be the spring cleaning of the soul that you much need, but there's a healthy way to achieve the same end, through self-awareness and conscious living.

▶ **Mental illness** What constitutes mental illness in one culture is a sickness of spirit in another, possession by spirits in yet another, altered consciousness in still another. If you are western you may embrace the DSM and its many classifications, but try to remember it *is* a work of fiction— the attempt of children to understand the unfathomable mind and spirit.

Too many things are being medicalized, theorized and categorized as illness. Recently a sixteen-year-old was acquitted of killing four people in a drunk driving incident because of *affluenza*; a term his attorney coined to denote someone too rich to know right from wrong. With that argument in mind, we'd have to empty all our prisons of the underprivileged due to *poorversion*. Every single crime ever committed could be acquitted through a defense of insanity by virtue of bad diet, bad parents, too much violence in movies, etc.

The difference between autism and a mental condition is that autism is neurological as opposed to purely psychological and is affected by physical attributes, and the differences are now virtually provable thanks to things like *brain mapping*. However, there are many possibilities for comorbid conditions when one is autistic, e.g. PTSD, bipolar, OCD, etc. Perhaps the biggest problem is the misdiagnosing of autism which leads to a plethora of labels, treatments and stigma being attached. From wrong therapy to medication to the wrong sort of interaction in the home and community, it's easy to go mad if you are misunderstood your whole life.

Likewise it is easier to be emotionally stable if you have never been challenged, if you never question the meaning of existence, or if you've had a relatively easy life. Sometimes messed up people are just the ones asking questions about themselves, the universe, etc. I'm not downplaying the reality of mental illness. I've met a few schizophrenics who have shown me that it is a real and heartbreaking condition. But sometimes I think that those who become mentally ill are simply the sanest ones in the room who were told so many times they were insane that they came to believe it.

There may be many reasons for mental illness, such as a traumatic childhood, traumatic events such as being in a war, being the victim of violence, tragic loss, or wrongful imprisonment. Things like these will take a lot of talking through with a professional or other experiencers, spiritual beliefs and counseling, and of course, love and support.

There may be internal physical reasons for mental illness, too many to list here, but a few are: candida, thyroid imbalance, mercury toxicity and vitamin deficiencies; diet can also be a huge factor. Any doctor who diagnoses a person with mental illness and/or prescribes psychotropic drugs without checking for things like this first is not doing his or her job properly.

▶ **Mimicking** All children learn by mimicking. Autistic children do it longer, sometimes well into adulthood. This is one of our gifts. How many of us do a really good Ace

Ventura, Pee Wee Herman, or in my case, virtually all of the Munchkins? In school we may fixate on a particular friend, and imitate their vocal inflections, choice of words, gestures. This can cause problems for us, obviously. It can be disconcerting to the one being copied, especially since we may be unaware that we are doing it, and are probably staring quite a bit to assimilate their traits. We must teach autistic children that they can be seen, as this is a problem for us—I can't see myself, so because of lack of social imagination, I don't realize others can see me. Talking to us about identity and letting us know that we do have a personality of our own can be helpful, as many of us don't feel like we have one when we are young. We may feel like blank slates, and we'll try to fill that slate with every character we come across that appeals to us.

▶ **Misdiagnosis** (and/or how do I know I'm really on the spectrum?) So far there is no definitive test for autism and Asperger's. The reality is, most of us will never have our diagnosis carved in stone. The problem of misdiagnosis is that we don't get the right treatment and approach, both formally in terms of therapy, meds, protocols, and informally in terms of expectations and labels.

Many of us have had the stigma of having several separate diagnoses of mental illness at various times in our lives, by doctors who did not put two and two together to make one diagnosis of AS. We may have internalized quite a bit of that with lasting repercussions. After we do receive an Asperger result, we may at various times in our lives doubt it ourselves, especially if we improve through the various methods mentioned in this book, or others.

I am not sure if I'd have Asperger's if I wasn't injured, neglected and frightened as a child and especially as an adolescent. Although I *clearly* remember autistic behaviors, e.g. fixating on patterns, music and stories, late verbal development, little professor syndrome, stomach issues, echolalia, etc., I also suffered a pretty serious head injury at eighteen months and brain injuries can mimic autism, as can the trauma of abuse and neglect. There is a very interesting article on this at the Child Welfare Information Gateway called *Long-Term Consequences of Child Abuse and Neglect.*[27]

Two things I've said before that warrant repeating:

- There are no penalties for applying autism-friendly advice in your life. It is universal advice for the most part, so if the information helps, use it.

- If you do not feel satisfied with your diagnosis, find someone who is truly expert in the field, such as the staff at Minds and Hearts (Australia) or others who work in or are aligned with autism/Asperger's organizations like the Asperger/Autism Network (AANE) (US) and who are *reputable*. Beware internet cowboys keen to dish out AS certificates at a price. I had one of those and have regretted it ever since.

▶ **Misunderstood, being** (see *Gossip*) Being misunderstood ranks at the top of the list for things people on the spectrum experience and dislike the most. As difficult as it is for us to understand others, it is just as difficult for them to understand us. So, what do people do when they don't understand something? Well, if they're intelligent, kind, truth seekers, they might try to gather information, get to know you. If they are lazy, presumptuous and gossipy, they may just fill in the blanks with behavior and traits that they can relate to.

It has shocked me (and many of you, I'm sure) how often I've been accused of doing things that are simply not within the realms of my thinking: lying, stealing, promiscuity, and a number of acts that I am virtually incapable of doing, as they either wouldn't occur to me, or I know them to be wrong so they would never be a viable choice.

Some people can be reasoned with, and you can tell them about yourself and they will listen. Others never will and will stick to their own toxic thoughts. If there's one thing I find incredibly poisonous, it's people saying, "You know what *you* are..." or "I know *all* about you," or "*You* think (fill in the blank)." No one knows all about you, no one knows what you think, and no one knows who or what you are better than you.

When you try to defend yourself with statements such as "Other people like me," they will say things like "They don't know you like *I* do," instead of realizing that we all have dark and light facets and that some people see the good in you.

This is often justification of their own bad behavior. In other words, they're treating you badly right now because "you deserve it, you brought this on yourself." Sometimes the person doing this is being bullied themselves and they're looking to vent their pain on someone else. It's a vicious cycle.

If you are experiencing this sort of persecution from someone, here's an affirmation that will help: "I am (fill in your name) and though I've made some mistakes, the good things that I've done and continue to do shall more than redeem me. And though there will be those who judge or misunderstand me, the bird's eye view of time will make it all, my motives and intentions, so very clear."

Here's another simpler one to take as your new motto: *Never complain, never explain.* We will all be misunderstood from time to time; it's part of life. Just be the best person you can be. The truth will come out, eventually.

▶ **Money** is a necessary thing. Humans, whether on the spectrum or not, fall into one or more of these categories: 1. we don't understand its value; 2. we have little or no financial sense; 3. we have good budgeting and accounting skills; 4. we are obsessed with the acquisition of more.

If money matters are an issue for you, as they are for me (I'm number two on this list) then what can we do about it? Spend our days praying for rain and a bumper crop? Or search for additional ways to make money and manage what we do have? Considering we can be so pragmatic about many things, we can also rely a little too heavily on magical thinking at times, nowhere more so than when it comes to love, career and money.

Making friends with money management, keeping the coffers filled to a healthy level, won't make you less autistic, but it will make you feel less stressed. There are few things worse than an empty cupboard, unpaid bills and red notices coming in the post. Create a game plan for earning and saving (see *Employment and self-employment*).

Write it down in black and white. How much do you have, how much do you need, how are you going to get it? This can be done for the short term, as well as long term. Use pen and paper, spreadsheets, or more sophisticated accounting software. (Simply search "best personal finance software" and have a look at some comparisons.) Next year you will be ready at tax time, with your numbers all neatly at hand, instead of being buried under a pile of receipts and despair.

Besides tax time, there's also the freedom of knowing that you will have enough to make your bills without having to do any last-minute hustle. Nothing puts a spring in your step like a cushy bank account and an inbox devoid of "overdue" notices.

If you are paid weekly or monthly, or are self-employed, your methods of budgeting will be different but the goal is the same: to take care of yourself, and that includes lowering your stress levels. Those of us who grew up in impoverished households might have inherited a "crisis-budgeting" mentality, which may make us swing in polar opposite directions—being totally tight-fisted or waiting for the hammer to drop before we pay a bill. Somewhere along the line, I learned that to pay bills with gratitude and a feeling of accomplishment is much better than doing so grudgingly.

▶ **Monologuing** (see *Conversation*) This autistic trait has a plus side, but when unchecked, it can be socially damaging and isolating. Our ability to orate at length about things we are interested in can make us riveting public speakers and good teachers. However, the same trait in a casual, social situation can make a person appear self-absorbed and a bit of a bore.

We are all prone to doing this. Sometimes, after a long day spent in our heads, the arrival on the scene of another person can open the flood gates and a litany of our thoughts spills out until it's spent, and then we can let the other person talk. My last partner and I had a deal that I would be allowed to monologue for a few minutes when he got home from work, then I would ask him about his day. Since I'd been home writing alone all morning, and he had a much more social occupation, it seemed a fair deal.

In everyday exchanges, with friends, strangers or acquaintances, we must really try to keep this trait in check. I've had to tell spectrum friends that they were monologuing, after several minutes had gone by and no one else had got a word in. It wasn't meant to hurt them, just to make them aware of their actions. On many occasions, those people, however taken aback, told me they weren't aware of this habit and thanked me for pointing it out. When you monologue at someone, Aspie or non, it can give them sensory overload. Being considerate of others and cultivating the fine art of listening are the keys to overcoming this trait.

▶ **Motivation and self-motivation** It's no secret to anyone related to or working with someone on the spectrum that it isn't always easy to tell us what to do. Motivation turns the key that starts our engine. Without it, we can have the best machines but they'll just sit there. Some people, on or off the spectrum, are go-getters, others are a bit more sluggish. There may be many reasons for this, from health, diet, depression, addiction, to going through a rough patch, finances, etc.

If you find yourself giving many reasons for why you *can't* do something, you may be falling into a negative pattern of thinking. Perhaps your energy would be better directed at what you can do and what you'd like to do as opposed to what you can't and don't. Not that you should ignore your aversions. When I wrote *Asperger's on the Job*,[28] I created something called the "personal job map" which utilizes both a person's likes but also acknowledges their aversions or triggers, to help guide them into the right career path.

The other purpose of the map was to self-motivate. We tend to be know-it-alls, so game plans we come up with ourselves are more likely to be acted on than those imposed from without. Of course, many of us take rules, instructions and orders very well; I'm talking more about our game plan for life than the minutiae of everyday college or work tasks.

Give yourself deadlines to accomplish tasks; they can be so motivating I prefer to call them lifelines.

For those of you who are parents or coaches and who are getting frustrated, it is better to find out what motivates us, what we want, and get us to tell you how we are going to achieve it. Offer your help if needed, rather than dictating. While I don't agree with the term *oppositional defiant disorder*, which is simply contrariness, we can be a bit contrary, especially if pre-diagnosis and still a bit un-self-aware as to just how AS affects us.

Last word on motivation or lack thereof, there may be some correlation between social media, video games and binge-watching, and not getting off our couch-shaped bottoms and actually doing things. If you spend hours a day playing games, being on Facebook or watching back episodes of *Game of Thrones*, look around. Is your house a mess? Are your children being ignored? Are you making healthy meals? Have you engaged in your passions lately? There's more to life than being online. Much more. No one will ever say on their deathbed that they wished they'd spent more time on Facebook.

▶ **Mutism** (see *Selective mutism*)

N

▶ **Narcissism, egocentrism and Machiavellianism** I do subscribe to the belief that many people on the spectrum (and off) display both egocentric and narcissistic personality traits. It may be difficult not to cross that line; to know where "healthy narcissism" or healthy self-love (as suggested by Freud) ends and unhealthy self-obsession begins.

If we don't get what we need in early childhood, e.g. if we are raised in institutions, or in a dysfunctional household, there will be defects in our ability to love and be interested in other people. When you add autism to the mix, this becomes exacerbated, because we do love our own thoughts, and we don't need the same amount of socializing as others do. But the distinction between autism and these disorders lies in a few things, such as: can we take criticism, and do we care about other people beyond how they "serve" us.

Both egocentrics and narcissists believe they are the center of attention. The egocentric, however, does not receive gratification by their own admiration, nor do they need the approval of others as a narcissist does. For the Aspie, sometimes *our seeming* egocentrism or narcissism is a misguided attempt to connect. We may appear self-centered while relating someone else's experience to our own. That's often how we generate understanding and empathy. Similarly, those who are self-employed, or creative in some way, such as artists and writers, may appear to be very self-centered even if they are not; they may be promoting their work for artistic or financial survival, not for personal aggrandizement. It's often difficult to tell a person's motivation.

Recently I've become much more aware of how destructive narcissism can be, and how vulnerable some of us more guileless Aspies might be to becoming victim to a narcissist. For narcissists are victimizers; they can be charming, exciting, seductive and many other qualities that serve to lure in a never-ending supply of fodder for their fragile egos and empty souls. While not everything with narcissistic traits has full-blown NPD (narcissistic personality disorder), if you do fall victim to one of these spiritual vampires, you may need counseling or help recovering from it.

Machiavellianism is "the employment of cunning and duplicity in statecraft or in general conduct." A person with this trait has a tendency to be unemotional, and is therefore able to detach him- or herself from conventional morality to deceive and manipulate others. Unfortunately, we do see people like this being misdiagnosed as Asperger's because of some overlapping traits.

▶ **Negativity and chronic complaining** Small children on the spectrum are going to be uncomfortable physically and mentally, from sensory issues, gut issues and social confusion. If your child complains a lot there is probably a reason and if you are the parent or a professional it is your job to come up with solutions. Some will be easy, e.g. cutting tags off of clothing. Others will take medical tests, diligence and the sleuthing skills of Sherlock Holmes.

When we get older, complaining and having a negative outlook on life may have become habitual without us realizing it. As a teenager, other kids made fun of me for it—they couldn't know what an unhappy home and internal life I had and how uncomfortable I was all the time. But as an undiagnosed adult this was pointed out frequently as well. At some point, I realized that I didn't want to be seen as a negative person. While we are not usually going to end up being cheerleaders and weather girls, we can rein in negativity by accentuating the positive in our lives. The truly inspiring person is not the one who has always had it easy, but the one who has had it tough and has learned to ride adversity like a skilled jockey. Practicing gratitude is one of the most powerful methods for overcoming negativity.

Negativity repels people, plain and simple. As my grandmother used to say, "You'll catch more flies with honey than vinegar." Of course as a literal Aspie child I didn't want to catch flies, but now I see her point.

▶ **News programs** (see *Asperger's: In the media*) Aspies can be pretty obsessive. News watching can become as compulsive as anything else and can feed our negativity, especially now that it's available 24/7. Like food, news should be taken in small quantities and it should be of the highest caliber. Papers like the *New York Times* are pretty trustworthy and have great websites for a small subscription fee.

Children today are dealing with more "news" that can feed PTSD and depression more than any other generation. If you or your spectrum child are feeling disheartened by things like climate change or a million other bits of bad news, do something about it. Whether it's a tree-planting project, a beach cleaning sweep, inventing another clean fuel or a million other options, empowering yourself rather than sitting back bemoaning the sad state of affairs will do wonders for your mental and physical health…not to mention the health of the planet.

Spend your time doing something that you enjoy: it will do a lot more for your life than being bogged down by mostly useless information.

▶ **Neurotypicals (NTs) or non-autistics (NAs)** You'll see these phrases throughout the book and in most literature on autism and Asperger's. They denote anyone not on the spectrum. I prefer non-autistic, because let's face it, no one likes to be called "typical."

▶ **Nightmares** (see *Sleep issues*) Western thought says that nightmares can be caused by traumatic events, stress, anxiety, PTSD, unexpressed negativity, physical discomfort, illness, medication, drugs and alcohol. Buddhists and others include spirits as possible causes. Some cultures think the placement of the bed can cause nightmares (*feng shui*).

Some dreams may be prophetic and our current level of scientific knowledge will not explain that, dismissing them as coincidence.

Whatever the cause or reason, when a person has frequent nightmares, it is considered a psychiatric disorder. (What isn't these days?) If your child is having nightmares, seek the source. This book lists countless sources of stress, physical, mental and emotional. If not diet or drugs (popcorn before bed seems to be a common trigger), there may be events in his or her life causing undue angst. Ask. The whole "How was school today?" approach to conversation with kids is not usually very successful at prying open tight lips. The website Aha! Parenting has some great tips on getting your child to talk.[29]

If you are the one having nightmares, put on your Sherlock cap and get to it. Like a person with stomach issues who spends their whole waking life in pain and doesn't realize it's not the norm, the chronic nightmare survivor might not either.

▶ **Normal** (see *Abnormal*) The only thing that determines "normal" is majority rule. Nothing else. A synonym for normal is ordinary, and really, who wants to aspire to that?

Having said that, some anomalies or abnormalities are positive—for example, creativity and eccentricity usually go hand in hand, and eccentricity can be wonderfully stimulating. Others can be jarring, off-putting or useless to you in the long run. It's up to you to decide what to hang on to and what to cast away. Personality traits, while deep-seated, are no more carved in stone than you are made of stone.

▶ **Nostalgia** There's good, healthy nostalgia and there's clinging to the past. Good nostalgia is when you take out the old photo albums (or old laptops), dust them off, and have a nice meander down memory lane. Or you spend time watching old films, reading old books or listening to old music, partly out of enjoyment but also to honor the arts of the past that have helped create the present. Calling old friends on the phone who you haven't seen in ages can be healthy and comforting to both parties.

But then there's living in the past, to the detriment of your future. Thinking that the golden era is gone and there's no point going on. Nostalgics like that are very similar to those of us who would rather live in Middle Earth than here. It's fine and fun to indulge, as long as it isn't escapism from the facts, challenges and realities of life. How can you have a future if you are only looking backwards? Even those who deal in cosplay events, antiques, swing dancing, etc., are plying their trade in the *now*. I have a theory, it's not very nice, but you know when you see people who have really outdated hairdos that they've worn since high school? It is because they are hanging on to what was probably the best time in their lives. A true child of the universe is forward-looking and not clinging to the past, no matter how good or how awful it was.

▶ **Obesity** (see *Diet*, *Exercise*) can be caused by genetics, medication or various diseases such as Cushing's, but other times it is the result of inactivity and bad choices. This is an inflammatory subject and I apologize for my candor. I'm not a doctor or nutritionist. I'm an observer. I live in an area rife with obesity, and the only restaurant choices here consist of pizzerias and burger bars, the kind where bigger is better and quality is of little account, where greens mean the bit of iceberg lettuce you get on your slab of greasy meat, where winters are long and harsh and staying active is difficult. If you are obese and you fill your shopping cart with potato chips, donuts, cookies, bulk candy, pop (diet being the worst), ice cream, absolutely everything that should only be eaten as a small occasional treat, that is a situation that can be solved through food education and awareness. If your idea of exercise is walking to your car, that, too, is a product of modern life.

You are doing yourself harm if you are filling your body with bad food and not exercising the machine you've been given. Some of you will be obese from childhood and will have had a hard start in life. But where there's life there is time for change.

What I remember about my own childhood is that there were virtually no obese people. Obesity rose with the availability of fast food and ready-made snacks. When I was a kid, an apple was a snack. There were no McDonald's, Burger King, none of that. As they appeared, our waistlines disappeared. Aerobics in the '80s kept us fit, but that was a fad that went the way of all fads. The fast food, however, kept coming. Portions got bigger and bigger and so did we. The solution? Don't buy it. Don't buy any of it. Ever. Eat real food, prepared by your own hands. Grow it if you can. Some of you work and commute long hours which make things much more difficult. In that case, finding restaurants or stores with healthy prepared food is a must. You can also spend a day or evening per week preparing things in advance, like soup, chili, gluten-free bread, pizza, casseroles, whatever. Keep a big bag of washed greens and fruits so that they are readily available.

Don't know how to cook? Use the internet; it's there for things other than looking at pictures of dancing goats and naked actresses. There are many recipes in the world that are tasty *and* healthy. Take up exercise. Even if house- or snowbound, if you have two working legs, you can jog in place, dance, bounce on a Pilates ball, whatever. Even those who are in wheelchairs may have some recourse to exercise their upper bodies. I don't mean to be cruel, but if you don't respect and care for your body it will eventually turn on you.

▶ **Obsession** The DSM-5 states that autistic people have have strong, focused interests that tend to be more heightened than non-autistic people.[30] That really puts a negative spin on it. Just think if Mozart wasn't obsessed with music or if J.K. Rowling wasn't fixated on writing about a boy named Harry Potter. Our obsessions give us *raison d'etre*, keep us busy, and may hold the key to our future careers.

Of course, it is one thing to be obsessed with information and activities. It is quite another to be obsessed with people. The latter is dangerous and could get you in trouble, either by getting a reputation, being rejected by the object of your obsession, or even getting into trouble with the law, i.e. having the police called or receiving a restraining order.

As with soothing behaviors, the key is *replace don't repress*. Channel obsessions into things that delight, enrich and hold possible career or financial promise. If obsessed with a person, the transition won't be easy. You will need to talk to someone, perhaps professionally, and you will go through withdrawal, but it can be done. All I can say is Auntie's been there. I want those years back which I wasted dreaming about what might have been. This is one time you really do need to get selfish, and love yourself more than the object of your obsession. You will be with you forever, and only you will pay for the time wasted. Spend it wisely. Information and education, unlike people, will never leave you.

▶ **Obsessive compulsive disorder (OCD)** According to the National Institute of Mental Health, OCD is an anxiety disorder characterized by recurrent, unwanted thoughts (obsessions) and/or repetitive behaviors. Most of us on the spectrum will have bouts of it in our lives. It may take the form of going back ten times to check the light is off, not stepping on cracks in the pavement, prodigious nose-mining and more. Some of these are perseverations, some are soothing behaviors (stims), some are embarrassing, others are debilitating. They all can be time-consuming.

If your OCD habit is getting you down, you need to enact a little discipline on yourself. I have a mental gate that I slam down, kind of like a garage door, or a portcullis if you lean towards medieval imagery. For example, I used to have bulimia when I was a girl, which many of us do experience at one time or another. In order to stop this life-threating condition, I had to slam the gate down on that behavior, as if it were an invasive intruder trying to rob me. And OCD habits do rob us—of time, of self-respect and sometimes of money, health, etc. So treat any unwanted thoughts and behaviors like the pesky critters they are. You wouldn't let a mouse come in your house and rummage around in your cupboards, you would do something about it.

Sometimes external, professional help is needed, in the form of therapy. Other times, you just need something to occupy your mind and your hands; as the old saying goes, idle hands are the devil's plaything. Written notes or checklists telling you to do or not do something are also helpful. Seriously. You can put one near the stove, saying, "Turn this off before you go and don't come back to check," and it may help break the habit.

P

▶ **Paranoia** is an irrational fear that someone or something is out to get you. It is very easy to be paranoid in this post-Snowden age, where we find out what some of us suspected all along, that the government, after eroding our rights, then abused their own to spy on all and sundry. I do not subscribe to the "if you have nothing to hide then you have nothing to fear" attitude that some have. I want my private conversations to remain just that. But if you think your every move is being monitored just because you posted a radical thought on social media or a video about UFOs, you're probably being paranoid.

I don't know if people on the spectrum are any more paranoid than anyone else, but if we are, part of our AS paranoia may arise from the fact that many of us were the odd ones out; we were gossiped about and ostracized as children, adolescents, and well into adulthood. We can perhaps then be forgiven if we think every office snigger and whisper is about us. But we do ourselves a disservice if we jump to conclusions, something a paranoid person can be very good at.

If you are prone to conspiracy theories and that sort of thing, at least do two things: *compartmentalize*, and put fears and suspicions aside long enough to get on with your day, your life, your work; then, take everything, even things you think you know, with a *grain of salt*. Illusion is a part of life. You can see a magician saw a girl in half with your own eyes, but you know it hasn't happened. Sometimes our eyes and our minds play tricks on us. Being 100 percent certain that something you suspect is true really does paint you into a corner.

While I'm tempted to be humorous and say, "Just because you're paranoid doesn't mean the world isn't out to get you," unless you're a spy, whistle-blower or terrorist, it probably isn't.

▶ **Parenting** (see *Step-parenting*) Babies. It seems a lot of people are having them these days. Aunt Aspie is not very sentimental. Instead of teddy bears and balloons, I'm reminded more of poop and pee and throw-up, because that's what your life consists of for the first couple of years. They are also very expensive to feed, clothe, maintain and educate, and they mess with every sensory issue known to exist.

They are also absolutely unbelievably gorgeous little creatures. All of them.

Once you have them, and I do hope you give it considered thought first, they are humans that you are in charge of developing. You *must* love them, and have fun with them and teach them things. I've heard of too many women and men who think they just can walk away, but bringing another human into the world is a magical feat and a hugely important task; the biggest karmic task of all.

One thing to avoid is having babies because that is the one major accomplishment in life that might be under your control. We may never get the career or life we want, but we can have babies. Not the best motivation. If you want someone to love, you might start with a puppy to see how well you do with feeding, vet bills, hygiene, and so on. It's a serious enough commitment, but at least you won't have to put it through college.

Cautions aside, parenting on or off the spectrum can be incredibly rewarding. You will have a little community of two or more, to teach, to share with and to enjoy; an oasis from the big strange world.

However, it cannot be said enough, having children will be very demanding and time-consuming, much more than anyone who has not had children yet can imagine. The demands that come with raising a child—shopping, cooking, cleaning, school demands, extracurricular activities, friends, temptations of adolescence, choosing and paying for college and so on—it really is a lifelong journey. Parenting is not a simple thing unless you live on a deserted island and your biggest decision will be mangoes or bananas today.

Having children will bring you out into the world in ways you relish, or in ways you might not want to repeat. I derived little pleasure from visiting my daughter's high school because my own experience in secondary education was so traumatic. But everyone is different. You may delight in every aspect of it, especially if your own upbringing was relatively happy.

Having control issues is something that will rightfully be challenged as a parent. You may think there's going to be two hours of classical music and two hours of reading and only macrobiotic cooking in your child's daily life, and then next thing you know, snack packs are scattered about while cartoons blare from the television and you're sitting there dazed, craving conversation from anyone who doesn't require nappy changing.

When you have Asperger's, parenting is complicated and intensified because you have the whole meltdown threshold coming into play, and may have children on the spectrum with their own meltdowns. You may want to impose dietary restrictions on yourself and your autistic children, such as GFCF, and may find that difficult with peer influences.

Having non-autistic children may take some cultural exchanging as well. Good communication, a sensory room in your house and respect for differences is paramount. Also finding a friend or relative who you can turn to for non-judgmental advice when you need it will be invaluable.

It's safe to say that some on the spectrum might find confrontation or emotional discussions difficult. One cannot be passive as a parent. Leaving important decisions to others with "Ask your mom" or "I don't know, what does your father say?" is confusing to a child. Every parent needs to be actively interested in the internal and external life of their child.

Love your children well. Play with them. Enjoy them. Give them a happy life. If you do your best, they may still find fault with you but love and truth will reign. Besides, someday you might need *your* diaper changed.

▶ **Pedantry** (see *Know-it-all*) is the act of giving too much unasked for information and being somewhat annoying in the process. The pedantic person may have a sincere wish to be helpful but if advice is unsolicited, one has to wonder if the pedant is just looking for opportunities to monologue and impress. Unfortunately it does not give a good impression and instead makes them appear self-centered, if not bombastic. One example: I recently asked people on social media, "Do you like your country and if so, why?" Many people misread the question and complained about their homeland, others recommended places they've never been. The pedant told me what immigration forms I'd need to fill out to live on their turf and even asked me my age to determine if I was a good candidate.

We all read into things…we hear what we think we hear, see what we think we see. It is good to try and really listen to what people are saying rather than imputing our own meaning on it (conclusion-jumping), which can get us into trouble.

▶ **Periods (menstruation)** No one likes them. They are a necessary part of being a healthy woman of child-bearing years. They come and go roughly every month a woman is not pregnant, so the average modern woman has 450 of them in a lifetime! One had better make peace.

Most youngsters on the spectrum are self-conscious and having their period will be a new and frightening thing for a young girl. We often have little or no idea what we appear like to others and may wonder if everyone can tell. Let me reassure you that there are things you can do to ensure this doesn't happen. First, never wear white or light-colored pants, skirts or shorts if you think you might be getting your period. Flying on a plane often brings on a woman's cycle, so apply this dress code to air travel. Second, bring a clean pair of undies in your purse for emergencies, and more spare tampons or pads than you think you might need. For a little extra security, you can always wear tight boxers over your usual knickers. Third, practice a few principles of good hygiene. If you are not one for a daily shower, make exceptions during your menses. We get stinkier than usual. Use deodorant at this time as well, even if you don't normally. Add a nice perfume (the organic, essential oil type if you prefer), just to give you that extra aura of fresh and clean.

Cramps are often present before, during and after menses (see *PMS*). They can be miserable things and are exacerbated by junk food, caffeine, lack of exercise, stress and more. Exercising and eating right before your period hits will help. It can also help during. If you are hit with cramps that could bring down an NFL linebacker (oh, these men have *no* idea), instead of curling up in a ball, go for a jog, do some aerobics, anything you can. Yoga can be good too, and while you might not relish the idea of someone touching you at this time, the right massage can be miraculous for cramps.

Most over-the-counter pain killers don't do much for cramps, but those created specifically for this purpose tend to work better. Midol is one, but be aware Midol Complete has caffeine, while Midol Teen formula, Midol Extended and Midol Cramps and Body Aches do not.

There are pills that suppress menstrual cycles, but I'm scared to death of them. It's not nice to fool with Mother Nature that much. Periods, like sweating, pooping and other body functions, are natural, normal ways of getting rid of toxins and things the body no longer needs. Stop that regular cleansing cycle and who knows what it might cause? I'm not a doctor but this is plain old folk wisdom.

Periods get expensive. Between you and me, after period number three hundred, you might get a little tired of splashing out for tampons. You can roll your own with a variety of materials, including unbleached cotton balls. You can also make washable ones, but you have to research the right materials to avoid bacteria problems. Saves you tons in the long run.

It is unknown whether we suffer worse cramps than non-autistics, but if we do, perhaps the cause is the hypersensitivity that is now thought to be a hallmark of autism, feeling things more than the average person, and perhaps hyperfocusing on the pain and discomfort instead of blocking it out. Of course, there are exceptions and many of you may not have this problem at all for a variety of reasons, including, but not limited to, a high pain threshold. You are the lucky ones.

▶ **Perfectionism** (see *Black and white thinking*) It is very difficult for some if not most autistics to do something less than perfectly. We may want to play violin and when we hear the awful scraping sound we make, throw it aside. We may not pursue sports because our first effort is less than prodigious. Many of us will therefore only pursue things that we have an instantaneous and natural aptitude for. Makes sense—stick with your strengths. However, it does limit us, and we may find that if we stick with something long enough (even sports) we can get just as good at it as the natural tendencies.

Part of our autistic program is geared toward perfection. Make the perfect design, write the perfect code, paint the perfect picture. When something is not perfect it seems to cause a software crash in our heads. This is why we are good employees and workers, but why we also overthink things like social conversations. Some things will always be subjective and for most things in life there is no such thing as perfection. Once we realize that, we can enjoy life so very much more, celebrate our accomplishments and raise our self-esteem. We are also less likely to be quitters.

▶ **Playtime** Imagine a world where children do not get to play. How sad it would be. Compared to how it was when Auntie was a lass, children don't play as much as they used to. The best therapy in the world, in fact, the only therapy for kids, was putting on your outdoor clothes no matter the weather and spending the entire day outside, laughing, screaming, running, jumping, swimming, skating, conspiring with your fellow small people. When it snows in my neighborhood, and that's happened quite a lot lately, I bundle up, and run around the house with my dogs. We take tea on the porch. We come inside, do tricks (the dogs, not me), read books (me, not the dogs) and roll around on the floor (all of us). I sing songs and play music for half my day. For most of my adult life, I tried to act like an adult and all I got was depressed. It's boring being an adult... responsibilities, bills, pressures. While those things come with the territory, nowhere does it say that we have to stop playing. Anyone who says that is just a crusty sad adult who lost their *joie de vivre* long ago.

Make time to play. Those with money may play tennis, go skiing, snowboarding, sailing, etc. but us less affluent folk can play too. There are plenty of things that cost little or nothing, a million things you can do to keep the kid in you happy.

▶ **PMS (PMT)** Premenstrual syndrome (or tension in the UK) is the time before menses, but you couldn't call it the calm before the storm, rather, the earthquake that precedes the tsunami. This strikes most women of child-bearing years and symptoms range widely from the physical to the emotional. Cramps, bloating, mood swings, backache, headache, food cravings, bowel irregularities, sleep differences and so on. There are many ways to combat PMS, from eating a healthy diet, to getting aerobic exercise and more. In her book *Girls Growing Up on the Spectrum*[31] Shana Nichols states that while there is no definite research to conclude that Aspergirls suffer worse with PMS than non-autistics, it appears that they may; whether it has to do with difficulty regulating emotion, sensory sensitivities, or something else, is uncertain.

The same advice for periods applies here. Exercise, diet and a plethora of other factors will lessen or increase severity of unwanted symptoms. In addition to the physical though, there's a verbal and even sometimes violent aspect to PMS. The Buddhists say the mind is a monkey that must be trained. Sometimes it's a giant ape. For ages there has been a tradition to medicalize and vilify PMS as an irrational state—to be avoided, if not voided—during which any opinions and feelings verbalized are to be filed under "disregard." While the feelings, thoughts and actions one undertakes in this hyper-hormonal state may be darker than usual, they may be the darker side of our true thoughts and feelings. I think this might hold more meaning for women on the spectrum who suffer from *selective mutism* or who are not comfortable speaking very often for fear of being branded strange. So for some females, the release of pent-up emotions during PMS is a real tidal wave that can literally knock people off their feet with its intensity.

We must learn to self-examine before acting out, and learn healthy ways of communicating until they become second nature so that when hormones take over, we don't fall immediately into a harsh and vulgar display of character. (I'm not saying you all do, but some of us will relate to this.)

We also should probably learn to respect and honor those thoughts and feelings that we do have during a PMS episode, as they may play out to be the ultimate truth, needing to be expressed. They may indicate actions that need to be taken, changes that need to be made; we just need the right amount of compassion for others to express them with restraint.

▶ **Pooping, peeing and other body functions** When I was a young child I found it very hard to poop. In his book *The Emperor C'est Moi*[32] autistic author Hugo Horiot says that he was afraid that if he pushed out his poop, his lungs would explode. It wasn't until something frightened him more—ending up in the hospital with intestinal blockage at age eleven—that he was able to master his fear. I don't remember what my motivation was (or lack thereof) but I do know that all body functions frightened and embarrassed me.

When I was five I was hit by a van and bedridden in hospital for several weeks. While there, I refused to pee and poo into the cold and undignified bedpan. Finally the doctors stuck a catheter in me and drew out my urine. They said they'd do the same thing to my butt if I didn't go. The thought of all those masked people pulling turds out of me terrified me more than the other option so into the bedpan I went. But my struggles weren't over. I couldn't pee in the toilet at school if other girls were in the room even though I was in a private stall. I couldn't even blow my nose if others could hear me.

The poop thing could be due to the intestinal problems that people on the autism spectrum are thought to have. But I think it was more psychological, an aversion to the meat locker my spirit was trapped in, an aversion to life, and at the same time, a fear of death. Even pulling on a turtleneck scared the crap out of me, as if it were a reenactment of my own birth.

As an adult, a lifelong struggle with pooping resulted in an abscessed and ruptured intestine which almost killed me last year, but I'm happy to say I've gotten quite comfy with sneezing and all the rest. I can even fearlessly don a turtleneck. If you and yours on the spectrum aren't going, you might end up having to pay the piper later. Diet (of course), gentle natural supplements, enemas, exercise, these are some of the things you can do to help pop out the poop!

▶ **Pop culture** The problem with popular culture is that it implies conformity. Once something gets big, everyone has to hear about it whether they want to or not. If you like pop culture, skip this bit. The rest of you... No matter how we try to avoid cheesy, nasty, popular so-called culture, it finds its way into our ears and eyeballs. When we walk through supermarkets we are still serenaded by the squeaky blandness of pop music, at checkout we have learned to look away from tabloids, to avert our gaze because the moment we read the headlines we can feel our IQ drop and spirit sag. When commercials come on our TVs, we rush to mute. We think that the bizarrely airbrushed-looking people on infotainment shows look like they came from Stepford and they frighten us. If you won't eat Mcfood, listen to McMusic, or watch McNews, this is not narrow-mindedness, this is having good standards. Just be aware that to judge others for it won't win you any popularity contests, so unless you're a blogger or critic, best not to make fun of others for watching *Pop Idol* even if the mention of it makes you want to find Simon Cowell and slap him repeatedly in the face with a dead fish.

▶ **Popular and unpopular, being** Pop culture says love yourself and don't give a toss what other people think, but then those who are different are told to learn to fit in, and on a much larger scale, society does nothing but push conformity on *everyone*: buy this, wear that, listen to this, watch that, use this new catchphrase. While I don't possess the secret to being popular, you can be happier (and consequently more popular) if you love yourself…but not *too* much. Take a genuine interest in other people, their thoughts and feelings, while not getting caught up in what they think of you. You can care what people think, without letting it dictate your actions. When you live this way, good people will come round. You might never host gala balls but at least people will be happy and receptive to see you when they do.

Those who are popular in high school often peak there, and the rest of their life is one long bout of nostalgia and reminiscence. If someone is popular in high school it's probably because they are good at acting like a high schooler. That has very little bearing on whether or not they'll make a good adult. In fact the better you are at being a teenager, the harder it'll be to let go of that mentality. You're only going to be a teenager for seven years, you'll be a person forever.

▶ **Post-traumatic stress disorder (PTSD)** Not every person on the spectrum will have post-traumatic stress disorder, but many will, especially if they were undiagnosed, unsupported, bullied or ostracized. PTSD is something that can happen after one suffers one or more traumatic events. The symptoms can include things like:

- Re-living the event: experiencing the physical, mental and emotional things that you felt while it was happening, such as a palpitating heart, fear, shortness of breath, etc.

- Avoiding things, places or people that might remind you of the event and trigger such feelings.

- Depression, anxiety, loss of enthusiasm, nervousness, jumpiness, trouble sleeping and more – these can all be residual symptoms of trauma.

As an older person, if you feel that over time you have acquired PTSD, either from a single event or, more likely, several, you have to approach it from multiple angles, since PTSD has mental and physical aspects. Everything in this book, from diet, to exercise, to monitoring our thought processes, to seeking therapy, establishing healthy relationships, etc., will all be part of the healing strategy. No one thing is going to get you whole. That's why holistic health (which should be spelled with the "w") is becoming so popular. We are a system of interrelated parts and subsystems. If one system goes out of whack, we can use the other systems to help it recover.

▶ **Poverty** (see *Employment*) Please excuse Auntie while she gets hot under her bonnet, but I know poverty. I used to love visiting my aunt's trailer because it was so much nicer than our derelict shack. Based on the evidence presented over time, I'm beginning to believe that there's an unspoken, unofficial (?) plan against the poor. When you look at the deterioration and destruction of affordable housing and the subsequent gentrification of places like New Orleans, San Francisco, New York, London, all the major cities, rich individuals and corporations are creating fortresses of ivory towers most of us will never be able to afford to live in. Many city jobs once held by the poor and less educated are now automated or outsourced to countries with cheap wages and few labor laws. The richest 1 percent now own more than 50 percent of the world's wealth. The seduction used is *be one of us*, the carrot that leads to all sorts of self-serving and dangerous behavior.

I believe the meek shall inherit the earth, but I wish they'd hurry up because the arrogant bastards have had it long enough. When I wrote *Asperger's on the Job*, it was difficult to get an accurate estimate of the percentage of the AS population who were without gainful employment, but the consensus was that it was very high, probably around 80 percent! Fact is, most of us will have a more difficult time getting a high-paying job with a steady pay check, whether this is due to self-employment, unemployment, only being able to handle part-time work, social difficulties, or comorbid factors such as health issues that make it difficult to keep a schedule. Hence, most of us will earn below-average income.

Asperger's on the Job is full of tips that can help a person find and keep their right livelihood. Poverty, like depression, is not our natural state but something that we may have a difficult time climbing out of. Truth is, you may have to work harder and smarter than your non-autistic friends. You may have to have more than one stream of income, a higher learning degree (or two) and become a master budget planner. Make earning money a special area of interest.

The real divide is not between races, or religions, or political parties. Those are just superficial distractions. It is not even between rich and poor, it is between greedy and not greedy, between those who are self-serving and those who have a social conscience.

▶ **Power** Finding your power can take time. Children have little, and adults can have theirs taken away by employers, society, diagnosis and stigma, by life's hard knocks, etc. As Aspies, not being known for subtlety or confidence, we might try to overcompensate with arrogance, steam-rolling our way through challenges. The most powerful people in the world are not those who toot their own horns all day talking about how great they are. More likely, they are the ones who plant seeds, then sit back and wait. They're often met with resistance, even from those closest to them, but they know in their hearts when something is worth fighting for. These are the ones who inspire us, the ones who make real change. Often, you never see them coming, or they are underestimated.

I've said it before, I believe a lot of depression can be caused by feeling powerless. The best antidote to that is action, but let it be mindful action. You will be in your power once you get to know yourself and, as often as possible, are true and authentic.

▶ **Probiotics** (see *Gastrointestinal issues*) are great for digestive health and, subsequently, autism. They contain more beneficial bacteria than yoghurt.

▶ **Profanity** It has come to my attention recently that some people think swearing, using profanity, is an indication of a person's character. I'm sure there are plenty of serial killers who never uttered a cuss word in their life, and plenty of good people (ahem) who frequently use profanity to blow off steam. If you are in the non-swearing category, that's wonderful, but don't judge others by its use. You really can't judge a dog by its bark.

I like to swear, and enjoy shocking people now and then. A cab driver once said to me, "Do you kiss your mother with that mouth?" I replied, "Yes. But I don't use my tongue." (Served him right for being cheeky.)

▶ **Proprioception** Have you ever thrown yourself down a bowling alley because you couldn't determine when to let go of the ball? Did escalators terrify you as a child, with their sharp metal teeth greedily awaiting your unwary toe or loose lace? Did you fall up stairs at bedtime? Have you gone to scratch an itch only to misjudge the distance and gouged your own flesh with a nail?

Proprioception is the ability to accurately judge where your body ends and everything else begins, and is something we Aspies often have an issue with. I think this makes us little Bodhisattvas, but not necessarily the most graceful ones. Certain kinds of exercise, sport and other physical activity can help you become more physically self-aware and aid with proprioception issues. Diligent practice will make you an ace at baseball or whatever else you set your mind to. It may not be fair that you have to work harder at such basic things as changing floors at the mall, but then again, not everyone can do what you do, either.

▶ **Prosopagnosia (face blindness)** Everyone has difficulty recognizing people from time to time, but for people with this condition/autism comorbid, it is often significant and can include not recognizing people you have had numerous encounters with. This includes family members and people you are intimate with, such as spouses, if you encounter them out of context. We even have difficulty knowing what we ourselves look like, at least to others. Faces tend to be segmented and contextual. You might work with a pianist with blond curly hair, see a pianist with blond curly hair playing in a club, and say "Hi," wave enthusiastically, buy him a drink and sit next to him on the piano bench before he looks at you and says, "I'm sorry, do I know you?" (Not that this has happened to me, mind.) You might see your sister antique shopping and not immediately recognize her, simply because you didn't know she'd be there. You might cordially thank a sinister ex for holding the door open for you at a supermarket and not realize it was him until you were halfway down the produce aisle. So you can see how this might get us into trouble. Similarly, you might encounter a boss or colleague outside work and not address them as they would expect, causing raised eyebrows, bruised feelings and potential judgment.

I've heard from wearers of Irlen lenses that they help tremendously with facial recognition. (So would regular glasses if you need them.) Meanwhile, if this is an ongoing problem for you, it's better to tell co-workers and friends that you have face blindness and that you may sometimes not recognize them. It's much easier than dealing with unmentioned bruised feelings from imagined slights!

Q

▶ **Questions** This is how a person on the spectrum gets information. We don't seem to glean information in the same way as non-autistics; i.e. from nonverbal signals, facial expression and body language. Children, particularly, will ask a new acquaintance many questions in order to get to know them a bit. This can make us seem precocious, mature and friendly as children, if not a little unusual. As adults it might be a bit jarring or inappropriate. We may seem nosey as opposed to just interested. Space your questions out, and remember that it's impossible to really know someone that quickly anyhow. True knowledge of another person is only acquired over a period of time. In addition, not everyone is honest so you can't believe everything you hear. Patience is key here.

▶ **Quiet** This is to our thoughts what a blank canvas is to a new painting, an empty cassette (for you old folks) to a mix tape. If you don't have quiet, how can you hear your thoughts? If you don't hear your thoughts, how can you know what it is you are supposed to be doing? If you live with an Aspie, please allow them to have some periods of quiet if this is important to them. Sensory overload is a real and debilitating thing.

▶ **Quitting** (see *Burning bridges*) I referred to this as *the pre-emptive strike* in my other books: quit before you're fired, leave before you're asked to, give up before you fail. Because of our tendencies toward perfectionism, we may give up on things before we've given them a fair shake. We may also develop a keen sense of impending trouble and think a situation is beyond hope or repair, so leave it prematurely. In addition, if we have had employment or social difficulties in the past, we may come to expect rejection and decide to quit and avoid the humiliation, thereby retaining some sense of control and dignity. There is validity to all these things, but the past is the past, and your story isn't finished. If we don't wish to repeat bad episodes in our lives, we either have to change our own behavior or gravitate to more appropriate people and situations. Most likely a bit of both is called for.

R

▶ **RAADS-R (Ritvo Autism Asperger Diagnostic Scale–Revised)** One of many tools used to assess Asperger's, it is meant to be administered by a clinician in a clinical setting. It is not meant to be a tool for diagnosis. Some clinicians, including the one who diagnosed me, used it as such, and I was told I "passed the test" halfway through. The whole experience felt unprofessional and unscientific. While my table of female AS traits, found in the appendix in *Aspergirls,*[33] is also used similarly, it never was meant to be used as a tool for diagnosis but rather an aid in identifying those who *might* be on the spectrum.

▶ **Rejection** This is something we may experience a lot of, and it often starts in gym class when captains are picking players for their team and we're the last ones to be chosen. Talk about wanting to crawl under a rock and hide! It can continue throughout school, for example if you don't get asked to the prom, or invited to social gatherings. It can continue into adulthood, not getting the job you want, or being fired from it. While we experience more than our fair share, it is a normal part of life to be rejected from time to time. A person who gets everything and everyone they want doesn't have much chance at building character. You do. The trick is to allow rejection to make you more empathetic and soulful, rather than dejected and bitter.

Your self-worth is being tested. At the end of the day, the validation and approval of others is wonderful, but it has to start with you. If you don't believe in you, why would others? After a lifetime, it can become second nature to expect rejection, but don't let that happen.

How we handle rejection when it occurs is also a big marker and test of our character. Don't expect rejection, but if it happens, and sometimes it will, do accept it graciously. If a partner breaks up with you, begging and clinging to their leg is not going to win you any points. Slamming your ex-boss is not going to ingratiate you with your potential new one, etc. When you handle rejection graciously, you will feel better about yourself, if not the situation. Congratulate yourself on being adult about it. However, if someone says, "It's not you, it's me," feel free to say, "I know."

▶ **Relationships** (see *Dating*) Starting with Disney and throughout our lives, films and songs will tell us that we are not complete without another person choosing us above all the billions of others of our gender to spend the rest of their lives with. No pressure. In the Bible, it seems to be given as some sort of divine task for women to find a partner (and some men to find dozens) or they are somehow flawed. My earliest daydreams involved marrying, alternately, Darren Stevens, David Bowie and Gomez Addams, and living happily ever after. I was certain that relationship bliss was right around the corner. Like with many Aspies, it has eluded me, for a variety of reasons, some clear, some unclear.

Of course, it is not just the media that convinces us we need to find true love. It is biology, pure and simple. We are made to conjugate. The search for friendships and especially romantic relationships may take a lot of the time and energy better spent elsewhere. Some more autistic people will not be interested in relationships, but they are further along the spectrum than most of us and far rarer than the seeker.

It is true that through relationships we are tested, and we might grow. Judging from many long-married couples I've seen, that isn't always the case. Some people are stultified, or they atrophy, finding it easier to settle into the belief systems and patterns that suit them as a couple. When you are alone in the world, you might find you have to be more open-minded, you will be challenged and you will almost certainly feel less safe.

Many of us don't want relationships, because they'll get in the way of all the lovely things we want to do with our time. And that's fine, and actually pretty considerate—if you know you're not going to be partner material, then good for you for recognizing that and sparing someone else a lot of pain and misery. Some of us are incredibly loyal and will stick with someone no matter how wrong for us they turn out to be. We may drive them away so that we don't have to be the ones to say goodbye. There are many potentials for mistakes and personal growth down this avenue. Let's break this down into a few categories:

Abusive A lot of crimes and abuse are committed in the name of love. This is not love. While what love does is difficult to define, here is what love doesn't do:

Love does not grab you by the throat and choke you to make you behave. Love does not punch you or kick you when it's angry. Love does not break up with you because you can't snowboard or rock climb well enough. Love doesn't alienate you from your friends and family in order to isolate you. Love does not text you sixty times when you're visiting someone else to say, "I love you"— that isn't love, that's smothering. Love doesn't lay around on the couch and make you do all the work because it's not macho.

Love doesn't badmouth things you love like family, friends, or anything else that is important to you. Love doesn't say, "They don't know you like I do," because you have friends. Love doesn't make you miserable, it makes you happy. If it does make you miserable, it's not love, it is some sort of mental enslavement. Vows are a two-way street, and if one partner breaks the "love and cherish" part, the contract is null and void.

I would rather be alone for the rest of my life than be with another person who subtracts rather than adds to the wholeness I feel inside and out. So for any and all of you, and I know there's quite a few, who are with someone who makes you feel bad about yourself, where's the good in that? Unless you have done something heinous, your partner should provide good constructive criticism that makes you feel enriched and excited, like when a teacher hands you a good book, not punished and humiliated.

Many of us have had it tough and have an underdog, *less than* mentality and might seek out the same. We all would like a bit of compassion, but if you go out with someone you feel sorry for, they won't feel grateful and appreciate you, but instead they'll see you as weak. Similarly if you make allowances for a partner's bad behavior, they'll see you as weak. It only follows that they would then put themselves above you. There can be forgiveness, but reconciliation can only come after acknowledgment and atonement.

In answer to the frequently asked question "Are Aspie/ Aspie relationships better than AS/NT relationships?" I have jokingly answered: they're both hell. Truthfully there is no pat answer, for every situation is unique. Just don't make the mistake of partnering with a non-autistic to give you validation and social standing. Many extreme non-autistics who like a wide variety of people will be attracted to us. In some cases, they might subconsciously be looking for a cure for their own extreme social needs. And for us, "See I'm not weird, so-and-so likes me" is not a good basis for a relationship and will lead to definite problems in the long run.

Challenges One of the biggest obstacles *all* of my relationships—both romantic and friendships—have faced, has been the opinion and intervention of other people. You can have the most understanding partner in the world who sees you for the wonderful person you are, but if his friends don't like you, it's going to put a massive strain on things. Before one of my partners and I ever got together he tried to make his best friend watch one of my YouTube videos.[34] She said, "I don't care about Asperger's, I want to know the real her." As if it was some hat I put on. She and most of his friends made absolutely no effort to understand me. Some of them seemed to dislike me either before they even met me or the very moment they did. It isolated us as a couple. I'm not sure there's an easy solution, but to be forewarned is to be forearmed. You could make an effort to befriend them, and help them get to know you; at the very least, you probably shouldn't say to your partner, "Your friends are idiots," because that's not going to give the warm and fuzzy feeling you might be looking for. Bald, naked truth is a bit harsh on the eyes and ears. Try making and keeping your own friends so you can each go off and play. At least you won't be relying on him or her to be your everything. There are many more challenges, but I've written two whole books on the subject; this is one I haven't quite covered before.

Rewards Having someone to eat with, cook for, cuddle with. Someone to help with chores and bills, someone to have sex with (safe sex, hopefully), someone to have and raise children with. Someone who gets you, respects you, prizes you above all others. Someone to travel with, go to a concert, museum, restaurant, play, whatever, with. Someone to walk in the woods with or in other places where you might not feel safe on your own. These are all practical yet idyllic benefits of coupling. It is likely that how much one does these things, and/or how much they are appreciated by the participants, will wane over time. The trick, I suppose, is gratitude, maintaining some independence (not clinging), and being realistic.

I want to add that whenever I'm speaking of couples, I'm referring to either gay, straight, or fluid. Addressing the additional challenges of same-sex couples is something I've touched on in this book, in entries like *Gender issues* and *Bigotry*. Since I myself do not care very much for gender restrictions, I do not feel compelled to go into it in depth. If you feel that there is a need to write a book about the unique challenges of being LGBTQ (lesbian, gay, bisexual, trans and queer) on the spectrum (or other minority), I wholeheartedly encourage you to do so, since I do frequently receive letters asking for such a work.

Last words: if you want to be with the one you love, love the one you're with…you!

▶ **Religion** This is not an issue that directly affects autism, but with so much religious fundamentalism (on all sides) growing all around, those of us with a fair dose of common sense and critical thought do feel penned in from time to time. There is a huge emphasis on religious conformity at the moment. One cannot drive through America without hearing preaching or singing about Jesus on more than half the stations. Think for yourself, decide for yourself, and remember that there are no flags in heaven.

Jesus was a pretty laid back hippy. In fact the only time I recall him getting really p.o.'d in the Bible was at the extorting money men. (I don't think he'd care for these televangelists very much, or all these capitalist banks that practice usury with impunity.) I don't recall a lot of judgment going on. And I've read almost the entire book. If you want to get fundamental, there's some pretty random things in there, like a recipe for goat soup that tells you not only how to make it but what day you should eat it on or you're committing sin. There are also schematics for building your ark where you need to store your frankincense. Funny, but I've never heard televangelists spouting that information. Lastly, I'm sick of religious fanatics blaming climate change on gays. They're blaming the wrong sort of Hummer. People who spout nonsense in the name of god are far more insidious than those who just spout nonsense, and far from being sacrosanct and off-limits, deserve to be called out.

At the end of the day, the law of karma is the only one we really need. Everything you do comes back to you, in this life or the next. When you realize that, you definitely think twice before hurting others.

▶ **Resistance** (see *Adversity*) There are two kinds of resistance one might get from the universe: the kind you should obey because you're on the wrong path, and then there's the kind that's just testing you. It's up to you to decide which is which.

▶ **Respect and self-respect** Respect is better than love in many ways. All manner of affronts, abuses and crimes have been committed in the name of love. Respect is consideration for another's time, thoughts, feelings and autonomy. Anyone can say they respect you, but actions speak louder than words. It is a key ingredient to any healthy relationship. Without it there will be dissatisfaction and sometimes even abuse.

People will respect you much more easily if you first respect yourself. I think one of the biggest challenges for Aspies, especially those from a dysfunctional family, is learning *self-respect*. We spend so much time trying to be like others, to make others like us, we're seen as odd, not worth taking seriously, easily taken advantage of. We may despise arrogance and strive toward humility, but instead end up devaluing ourselves.

Don't try to buy people with money or favors. Let those come to you who will. Do not go out of your way for those who are using you. Meltdowns often come after people take us for granted and disrespect us. Trick is to change our m.o. so it doesn't come to that. Call people and things out as you see them, instead of putting a fire on a shelf, only to have it burn your house down later. Be warned, once you have a meltdown, it will detract from others' respect for you. No matter how understanding they may be, you will be seen as "unwell" and it can take a very long time to undo that damage.

As far as relationships go, you can be as beautiful as a Hollywood starlet, but if you don't respect yourself, potential suitors will sense it and they may date you, sleep with you, etc. but they will never take you seriously. An unattractive person with self-respect is more attractive than a supermodel without it.

You may have had "sucker" stamped on your forehead in the past, but no more. Your psyche is nobody's shit repository, recycle unit or day care center.

▶ **Rest and relaxation (R&R)** We with AS can sometimes take too much on, because we like to be engaged.

And while some of my AS friends can be so dormant that chipmunks begin to perch on their heads, many are some of the hardest-working people I know. Fear of poverty, being dependent on others or the state, might make some of us workaholics. But taking time to recharge, rest, relax, snack, bathe and play, these are indulgences that are necessary for a balanced psyche. It is hard for us to turn off our minds, especially if we have eidetic or photographic memory, or have had a busy, overstimulating day. Taking some downtime will help us wind down towards sleep. It's also easier to connect with partners, children, friends and pets after sitting still and emptying our heads for a few moments.

▶ **Rigidity** Rigid thinking and behavior repels others, makes us seem inflexible and unteachable and is both isolating and exhausting. Loosening your mental bra will make you feel and appear freer and easier to get along with. Rigidity is usually a product of anxiety and wanting the comfort of the known, including rituals and routines.

▶ **Ritual and routine** (see *OCD*) Part of the criteria for autism in diagnostic manuals are the need for sameness, inflexibility in changing habits and routines and ritualized patterns of behavior (verbal or nonverbal). News flash, everyone has rituals and routines, from starting their day with a shower to ending it with a nightcap and a million in between. Get between a yuppie and his mocha and you just might see Louden blow his tie bar.

Some rituals and routines are sanctioned, normal and acceptable, especially if they involve legal drugs like caffeine. Other more unusual rituals are what concern us, and/or the frequency of their occurrence as well as the ramifications if they are unable to be performed. In other words, are they interfering with your ability to have a normal life?

Like any habit, there has to be a desire to change, and reward will usually be more motivating than punishment. When it comes to anxiety, ritual and routine, and OCD behaviors, as with all autism traits, diet should be the very first thing looked at. Other options:

- *Behavioral therapy*, formal or informal, may help you stop avoiding cracks in the sidewalk, flipping light switches, counting syllables in your head, etc.

- *Talk therapy.* This can help you figure out if there is some fear-based rationale behind the action and what the source of that fear is.

- *Mental discipline.* This is the hardest to pinpoint, to improve, to change. My friends on the spectrum who have discipline are much more fruitful, creative and successful than those who can't seem to organize their own thoughts and actions, who seem to have difficulty with executive function. In this instance, we must look for the source: is it depression, and is that diet-based, event-based, substance-based or genetic? Are there medications involved that might be causing problems? There are no easy answers, just a lot of questions to get you started. It is very difficult to motivate a person on the spectrum who doesn't want to change. We naturally reject being told what to do.

Many if not most rituals and routines are benign, and if they make us happy and aren't costing too much in terms of lifestyle, etc., then just let us have them without stigma. Stigma often just makes things worse. It brings shame into the picture, which creates anxiety, which exacerbates the need for ritual and routine…round and round we go, ad infinitum.

S

▶ **Savant** (see *Talent*) Someone who has an exceptional ability, taken to a prodigious level, while also having some cognitive or physical disability.

▶ **Selective mutism (SM)** is the temporary inability to speak. It is not the same thing as not wanting or choosing to talk, it is involuntary and usually accompanied by some physical paralysis and mental repetition of unpleasant thoughts, such as *they hate me* or *I'm such a jerk* or *just move, damn it!* It is a very debilitating and unpleasant thing for the experiencer and may be accompanied by other sensations as well, such as a painful throat, dizziness and deep shame.

I've read that most people on the spectrum experience seizures and many of these may be subclinical (not easily detectable or noticeable), and selective mutism may be a manifestation of that. It may also be an extreme manifestation of the *fight, flight or freeze reaction* that we have when we feel threatened. People on the spectrum have told me that SM is often triggered by a feeling that someone is being hostile towards them (this was my experience as an adolescent as well).

There are studies now which connect or connote mild catatonia with some of the traits of autism, including selective mutism, so some may consider this mild catatonia. SM was originally called *aphasia voluntaria*, suggesting it was under the control of the child, but trust me, it isn't. The DSM lists it as a disorder, and it is considered an anxiety disorder by many, but as with everything in autism, one must look for the biological connections; is there a seizure happening, and if so what can we do about those? Is there fear and social anxiety, and what can we do about that? And did we have a packet of Skittles for dinner or a nice pot of delicious healthy, autism-friendly food?

When a person experiences a bout of SM, it will take a while for them to return to normal. Remove them from the room wherein the upset occurred, or remove the person or circumstances that are causing the upset. Get them to a quiet place, offer cups of tea or whatever solace is required. Tell them that you are there when they are ready to talk about it. Ask if they want to write down their thoughts and feelings. Journaling our experiences can be an incredibly healing process. If you are the one who experiences SM, do the above for yourself. Have a bath, play quiet music, do some yoga or something that brings you back to a safe, even place. It is frightening to think we don't have total control over such basic functions as speaking, moving or thinking. Everyone, at some point in their life, realizes their own fragility. But you also have great strength. You will recover from this episode, and you will very likely outgrow these bouts of selective mutism; they rarely last very far into adulthood.

▶ **Self-advocacy** can range from speaking up for yourself when slighted, to fighting for your job back after wrongful dismissal. It is not an easy thing for autistic people to master, for many reasons. In the moment, slights often go right over our heads, as we are not usually quick to give them and don't expect others to derive pleasure from such an occupation. We generally don't enjoy confrontation, and also, we may get used to being the odd one out, the one not picked for the team, so that we may come to expect rejection.

Speaking up for ourselves is difficult. Even when we know that we are right, it doesn't really make it any easier for a sensitive soul. Yet speak up we must. For sometimes, the energy required *not* to say something may be enormous. Or the consequences may be dire, such as losing your income.

In the case of a slight or insult, first, we must take a breath, make sure we're not imagining or overreacting, and second, we must not spew venom or send angry emails in the heat of the moment (especially while drinking or otherwise intoxicated). However, when someone burdens us with something like a back-handed compliment or sneaky insult that makes us feel bad, sometimes we simply have to hand some of that burden back. A clever, humorous comeback is a handy thing. Keep some in your mental arsenal. You can also ask, "What did you mean by that? What do you think I meant? What was your motivation for saying or doing that?" There's always the possibility we might learn something and that we're not the angels we thought we were, or that our memories aren't as accurate as we believe.

When it comes to major issues, for example wrongful dismissal, or your counselor is caught discussing your private sessions on Facebook with strangers (happened to me!) then you might need to get legal on their butt. What you have to understand is that there is more than self in self-advocacy; speaking up against injustice may be helping the other would-be victims of the perpetrator.

I recently got so good at advocating for myself I began telling off everyone who looked at me sideways. The pendulum had swung too far. That's another thing to watch out for, since we are a people of extremes. Another thing to avoid is saying things to people online that you wouldn't say in real life. I call this flexing your i-muscles, the virtual equivalent of beer muscles. This is pretty cowardly, and possibly worse than the behavior you are condemning. Social media makes it easy to say things you are thinking, but it also creates a lasting record and impression of your character.

▶ **Self-centered and selfish** (see *Introspection*, *Narcissism*) Human beings have to be selfish to survive to some degree. What's the opposite of self-centered anyhow? Other-centered? How many people fit that bill, truly? We all have to bathe, feed and clothe ourselves before we can get on with the business of taking care of other people. For some on the spectrum, those first few things might be harder to do because of monetary reasons. Or because of depression. It's very difficult to think of others when we are in a funk. Ironically, doing things for others is one thing that might help us get out of it.

When you are a solitary creature, you get used to thinking in terms of "I" as opposed to "we." This is made all the more poignant and pronounced by the social isolation many of us feel, even in a crowded room. It's difficult to think of the crowd if they aren't nice to us, or welcoming, or if we feel intrinsically different from them. Just as one species of animal doesn't include another in his pack, we may not feel we are the same species as other humans. We may not feel we have a tribe of our own. That's why AS or special interest groups are so important if we don't naturally gravitate to, or have the opportunity to mix with, our "own kind." Once we have a tribe and feel like we are a valued member of a society, then we can be a bit more gregarious and reach out and even mingle with other tribes. We can become less navel-gazey and me-centric if we feel loved and valued.

Creative people on the spectrum can be seen as the most self-centered of all. Creativity usually requires a lot of time alone, spent in contemplation and then execution. Of course, once our work is created, we want to share it with others, so we talk about and promote it. The "self" is not really on our minds, but it might be how others see our actions.

▶ **Self-esteem** (see *Confidence*) The self-esteem of Aspies tends to vacillate between very low and very high. We can swing from abject humility to grandiose arrogance in a quick and surprising manner. This is for a few reasons, many of which we've discussed, and they all come together to form this stew: wanting to be loved and accepted, being told and feeling that we're different, having our differences medicalized, i.e., called a disorder. Yet we may possess higher fluid intelligence and/or other fairly impressive traits. We may be bossed, bullied and isolated, and feel physically unwell. We may want to make the world a better place and feel as if we actually have the capacity to do that if people would just believe in us and give us a chance. So, humble Harry might be quiet, modest and self-deprecating much of the time and then suddenly say something grossly arrogant.

Black and white thinking may also play a role in the self-esteem pendulum process. We did great, so we are great. We did badly, so we are bad. Learning that the moment does not capture the totality is very important. Understand that doing badly or great makes us neither.

You'll notice that we are not great at accepting compliments any more than criticism. We are perfectionists and may get annoyed at a compliment if we feel we did less than perfectly. Learning to accept compliments graciously is one good exercise for practicing healthy self-esteem, so is taking criticism. Do not allow the compliment or the criticism to define you, but simply learn from it or ignore it, whatever is warranted.

Accomplishments also play a role in self-esteem. If we are having a hard time holding a job and a home of our own, and feel like we're just treading water when we dream of big things, we will find it hard to be happy and confident. Set realistic short-term goals and record and *celebrate* each accomplishment in some way.

Healthy self-esteem comes with time, patience, acceptance, love and support, and accomplishments. Learn to celebrate your small victories and you'll pave the way for bigger ones to enter your life.

▶ **Self-improvement** The urge to self-improve might come from a problem that needs fixing, or an urge to better yourself. For a while, self-improvement was such a buzzword that it became more like self-indulgent self-worship, a striving towards perfection that no human could possibly muster.

In youth, we can place too much emphasis on the physical. I remember being twenty and striving towards a perfect body, makeup, hair, etc., and feeling constantly thwarted and negative. It was a constant source of angst which led to obsessive exercise, anorexia, bulimia and depression. I knew I was different and thought that if I was just prettier I'd fit in and get along with others better. Of course that was folly. I was very pretty—it was my self-esteem that needed improving; also I needed a diagnosis, with some information and help.

The media (American TV hosts and stars particularly) have taken the perfect body, impossibly white teeth, perfect hair, perfect noses and airbrushed makeup to such an extreme, they all look like androids. They tell us what book to read, what exercises to do, what foods to eat, all to aid us on our journey to perfection like them. They scare me.

An Aspie might rebel because of emphasis on the shallow (what difference does it make how you look?). Also because of the realization that perfection is not attainable. If perfection is not attainable, why improve at all? Self-improvement is not about reaching some plateau in life where everything is suddenly hunky dory and you will never have problems again. Self-improvement is about making the here and now a little better for you, and consequently for those around you. That's all. Nothing scary about it. Don't let the androids put you off.

Films and television have brainwashed us all into thinking that by the end of the third act, we'll either be dead or living happily ever after. Truth is, most of us will live a lot longer than we thought possible, and none of us will live happily ever after. The best we can hope for are many moments of happiness, and to hang on to our own teeth for as long as possible.

▶ **Self-pity** (see *Depression*) This is like the chocolate river in *Willy Wonka*. Murky, sweet, dangerous, seductive…and very difficult to climb out of once you fall into it. I, like many of you, have succumbed to the siren call of self-pity. We may have a lot to feel sorry about; if I describe my childhood and some of the events of my life as if talking about someone else, I'd feel very sorry for that person. In a way, that's a healthier way to approach the subject: taking a detached, empathetic view, but not internalizing the pity; saying, "Yes, that is terrible, but now, what can we do to make things better?" For that is what you would say if you were looking at a girl, boy, man or woman who needed your help.

And there is the remedy. The remedy, almost always, is action. Not reaction, not self-destructive action, but positive, proactive action. Bad health, bad marriage, no income, whatever it is, there is always *something* you can do. Be careful when interpreting this. If, for example, someone broke up with you, I'm not suggesting you go after that person. No, I'm saying do something that makes you feel better and empowered. Engaging your mind elsewhere might be the action needed.

If you have low energy and feel you need to slow down, meditation and contemplation are more positive ways of doing "nothing." In actuality they are doing something, as they usually involve specific thoughts or actions (e.g. breathing) that will focus the mind on the here and now. Journaling is another positive outlet that might lead to epiphanies and breakthroughs.

Admittedly, sometimes we need a good wallow: a day of inaction, lying on the couch, eating popcorn, binge-watching British crime thrillers, oh, how we do love those days.

But, you get one day. In the case of very serious episodes, you may get more. But one must have a deadline. Just as most of us go back to work on Monday morning, wallowing only gets a weekend pass. When it's time to show him the door, off he goes. Back to work, back to life.

All kinds of stuff, good and bad, is going to happen. You can't control most of it. You can only control how you handle it.

▶ **Sensory issues** The learned doctors who created the DSM-5 have finally put sensory issues into the criteria for autism. Kudos to them for taking decades to realize what every person on the spectrum and their parents have known since day one…stuff hurts! Lights, fabrics, smells, noises. I'm not going to list them all here; while there are triggers common to most of us, like fluorescent lights, e.g., we are all individuals. I love the smell of lavender but it might be like cowpat to you and so on.

There are also areas in which we are hyposensitive—some of us have a very high pain threshold—while hypersensitive in other areas. What we all have in common is a need for a sensory toolkit, which we take on the go, and a sensory room, or sensory-friendly house. It astounds me when people on the spectrum say they don't have these. For a child, their kit will be in the school backpack—either a separate pack within it, or a section of the bag. For women, it may be half your handbag; for a man, a backpack, briefcase, or man-bag. The things in it will depend on what your sensory *triggers* are. List them. Here's a sample of mine: traffic, wind, metallic noise, bright glaring light, ceiling fans, crackly speakers in stores, chemical smells, crowds.

What on earth could combat all those? You'd have to have Mary Poppins' magic carpet bag to fit an anti-wind machine in it, wouldn't you? Not at all. Here are the kinds of things that one could use:

Sensory toolkit A snug-fitting jacket with a hat that won't blow off, or a hoodie; headphones with favorite music; earplugs; sunglasses; sachet of dried flowers (or cologne if that's how you roll); smartphone, laptop or book; soft toy or stress ball.

The stress ball is not to throw at crowds, it's to give you something to do if you get stressed and want to fidget. Feel free to mess with this list. I also like to bring tea bags, and anything that will hydrate, soothe, de-stress.

I stand by this: if you eat a healthy diet, exercise and regulate your sleep patterns, you will find you are less sensitive to some of your sensory triggers, and that may even include the greatest trigger of all: people.

Sensory room A sensory room is a must for anyone on the spectrum who does not live alone. It could be your bedroom, but chances are your bedroom is full of clothes and things that could be considered clutter and have functional use, so doesn't exactly say "escape." A sensory room, however, might have fish, lava lamps, yoga mats, balloons, toys, posters of exotic places, fountains, etc. It must be a sacred space, and the person in it must be allowed to be in it without anyone shouting in at them.

Every school should have a sensory room. If an autistic child is getting overloaded in class, they may get disruptive. Yelling won't work, telling them to behave won't work. Asking them if they need a few minutes in the sensory room might do wonders for classroom management. If other children balk, remind them that it's very difficult being autistic and getting overloaded and how would they like to try that for a day? School doesn't have the room or the budget? It could be a converted broom closet kitted out with things from a dollar store; it doesn't have to be a Hollywood production. The main thing is to be away from prying eyes, noises and judgment.

▶ **Sex** (see *Sexual abuse*) It's messy, it's smelly, we don't know when to put what where (not the first time anyway), and it pushes all our sensory buttons, sometimes in the right way and sometimes in the wrong way. I think if you begin to resemble a traffic cop, referee or charades player in bed, you might be with the wrong person, or maybe you're just not in the mood, not ready, whether it's your first time or fiftieth. I don't think there's as much of an *AS/NT divide* as there is a *male/female divide*, a *those who want true love/those who want to get laid divide*, or a *those who are hypersensitive/ hyposensitive divide*. The trick is to know where you stand on all those things at any given time. Sounds like a lot of work. Shallow people must have it so easy, but then again, probably don't have the physical or emotional sensitivity to see the true beauty of a conjugal union.

Some religious or philosophical groups think that a person isn't complete unless they have coupled with another human and declared true love and fidelity. Others take the hermetic approach, that union clouds the mind, distracts from our higher purpose and inner divinity. I vacillate between the two. The truth is, as long as we are walking around in these meat lockers we call a body, we have needs. Physical needs. Most of us will be happier and more pleasant to be around if we get laid now and then. I feel about ascetics the way I feel about vegans—"Yea, you're all pleased with yourself, but you really look like you need a cheeseburger" (or sex, in this case).

Another issue, and I've mentioned this in other places, is how impressionable we are, and how other people's rules, beliefs, hang-ups and histories can impact us. If your uncle is an aunt-hater and your aunt is an uncle-hater, they might try to scare you with their own twisted tales of two-timing, and grubby late-night grapplings behind the bowling alley which led to your hateful cousin Billy Bob. Your church might tell you that your own homosexuality is wrong, even though you've been gay since you didn't want to see Jane running after Dick, you wanted to see John running after Dick. But you know your needs and your nature. As long as it involves *consenting adults*, it's probably okay.

Sex is like snowboarding. You have to try it at least once, but you won't be good at it unless you invest in a season pass, maybe get some lessons. But sooner or later, you'll realize whether you really take to those mountains, or if you're more the "I'll be by the fire with a good book and a brandy" kind of person.

Besides the creation of children, sex has a more immediate goal. The orgasm. It's the most fun you can have legally. Ever. If you don't know if you've ever had one, you've never had one. Your whole body heats up, engages towards the goal, and when it reaches climax, your genitals, the surrounding area and sometimes even your whole body pulsates with a powerful sensation… I mean, that's what I hear, anyway.

Using pornography and prostitutes (see *Sexism*) There are many sides to this issue. Many young men would never have the opportunity, the skill or the knowledge to be with a woman (or man) in bed, unless they sought their education from some graphic means, such as pornography, visiting their local strip club to see what a naked woman looks like in the flesh or hiring a prostitute to have sex with. In some places, the so-called oldest profession in the world (I think hunting and gathering probably came first) is legal, licensed and regulated. There are so many inherent or potential problems in this, however, that it warrants some address here.

First of all, there's a lot of illegal pornography in the world, and a person on the spectrum might not be able to understand the difference between legal and illegal video and images. Second, the objectification, slavery and oppression of women is a global problem. How do you know that the naked, smiling affectionate woman in the video isn't underage, coerced either through threat of physical violence or poverty, and has nowhere else to turn for an income? When it comes to strip clubs, Auntie has met many dancers; I was even part of the first unionization of dancers in the US in the late '90s. Some strippers and nude dancers genuinely like their job, others are lesbians who are ambivalent about men, and see it just as a job to pay for school or life's demands, and some genuinely despise the men who slaver and drool over them. Personally, I found that most of the women I met in that field had troubled upbringings, including sexual abuse and resultant self-esteem issues. Lastly, if you pay a woman to give you a lap dance or have sex with you, she is going to be very accommodating. It's her job. You might come to expect the same sort of obsequious and pliant behavior from women in everyday life.

The other issue I have is that there isn't the same opportunity for women to hire handsome young men without stigma. All of society, especially the underbelly of society, is geared towards pleasing men. If prostitution, the act of hiring someone to service your physical needs, ever gains widespread acceptance, I truly think it should be completely egalitarian and unisex. Let's face it, there are lots of single older women who are sick to death of watching Netflix night after night to get their dose of cutie booty.

At the end of the day, be honest, be legal, be safe and be considerate of the other person. And have fun!

▶ **Sexism** Yesterday I walked into a store where a lone woman "manned" the registers. A loud fella in a plaid shirt and dirty jeans strutted up to the register and shouted loud enough to fill the store, "Come on, smile. You should smile more." When I approached the register minutes later with my own shopping, I gave her a comeback. "Next time a man tells you to smile more, tell him to talk less." The other three women behind me practically applauded. We are all sick to death of being told by men what to do, bossily, without apology, while we have to be tactful and try not to appear bossy…god forbid.

A woman who looks serious is not doing her duty, apparently. Recently, some blithe gentleman posted a comment on my social media photo: "Oops, you look angry." *Oops*. In other words, if a woman commits the mortal sin of looking angry—i.e. not cheerful—it must of course be accidental because we just live to look cheerful. A friend of mine laughed and said I have *bitchy resting face*. His silly little *rude* comment carries within it millennia of the oppression of women: "Smile, look seductive, god forbid you should look like you have anything important on your mind. If you do you have problems—you must have done something to deserve it." Women area here to be the reassurers, the ones to say, "Let me make you dinner and a cup of tea and don't worry darling, everything will be fine."

Gentleman: think there is no sexism and both genders have their challenges? Of course they do, but the odds are still stacked in your favor. I'm a woman alone. No partner. Some women get more interesting and more successful on our own, but rather than being seen as distinguished, eligible bachelors we're seen as a pathetic *spinster*, which becomes a self-reinforcing state. Unlike a man, I can't go to the local pub, order a beer and shout out, "Who won the game?" without seeming like some desperate cougar out to be granny grabbed. I either have to find a single friend of a similar age (oh look, two cougars), a partner, or two gay men to accompany me, as I saw so many evenings in San Francisco: elderly ladies in diamonds and furs, two young gay gentlemen dressed the same, sipping cocktails and discussing the merits of Greta vs. Marlena. I could do that, but there isn't an openly gay community in my small hamlet of deer-stalker fashion, Budweiser and pickup trucks. (I do wish someone would start a match-making service for women of any age to meet gay men.)

Just try hiring a contractor when you're a woman alone. I once had a foremen lie to his employees about how much I paid, then try to sue me. I won of course, because I had receipts, but it was very stressful. Being alone in your house with two angry men with hammers leaves one vulnerable. I've had other men tear up floors and pull pipes apart, and then threaten to leave it like that unless I paid them more. I threw them out on their arses, but again, dangerous, stressful and time-consuming. Somehow I don't think those things would have happened if I'd had a strapping husband and son around.

A few requests of men: let a woman finish a sentence for chrissakes!! The last several potential suitors I've had have told me their life stories over the phone, but the moment I started talking about myself, my history or my work, they cut me off and brought it back to themselves. That's not to say they didn't compliment my work or my looks, but that's not the same as listening. I could hear their ears glaze over. If being in a couple means I never get to finish a sentence, I'll stay single. This is pervasive in our culture. In the film *London Boulevard*, starlet Charlotte says to Harry, "The role of a woman in films is to give the male lead someone to talk to about himself." As in art, so in life. Speaking of films, if you ever hear one movie trailer with a female voice-over, I'll eat my apron.

These are just tiny slivers of sexism in my little world. What goes on on a global scale is mind-blowing. We don't want to get into statistics for violence, rape and oppression the world over but here are just a couple of interesting ones:

almost all major politicians in the US are white men but white men only comprise 35 percent of the population. In the UK, 45,000 women vs. 5000 men got plastic surgery last year, mostly to work on their breasts—bigger for the women, smaller for the men. I'm gonna go out on a limb here, but let's be honest. Big boobs do nothing or little to enhance sexual pleasure, while penis size, on the other hand, is, erm, instrumental. If we objectified men's penis size as much as breast size is mentioned or exploited we'd have a lot of men walking around with their, erm, tail between their legs. That is, if it could reach.

Women still do not get equal pay for equal work; the Equal Rights Amendment (ERA) was never passed, and instead of women being prized for child-bearing capabilities, it is held over our heads in a number of ways—e.g. you'd lose the benefits afforded to your gender if the ERA was passed, was the argument. Young women today still do not have equality. (Being louder, trashier, brassier and letting men objectify you does not make you equal.) According to a study by the World Economic Forum in 2012,[35] using economic, political, education and health-based criteria, other countries have a smaller gender gap, including Iceland, Finland, Norway, Ireland, Sweden, New Zealand…even Lesotho! The US and Canada don't even make the top 20, while the UK just squeaks in. Tsk, tsk.

▶ **Sexual abuse** Recently in the UK there have been several high-profile cases of historic sex abuse—events that took place many years ago. I'm sure many if not most of these are legitimate and should be redressed. Here in America, each state has its own laws and statutes of limitations, so that people cannot press charges after a certain amount of time has passed. However, there is no statute of limitations on the psyche, and the lasting damage sexual abuse can do.

Sexual abuse can manifest in obvious form, such as forced penetration, but there are other things that are not as extreme, and these can also create lingering damage. The trouble with memories is that they remain in our hard drive somewhere, even if we can't access them consciously.

I'd been carrying around one such memory for years, and didn't know it until about a decade ago. But recently, at the ripe age that I am, I've realized what an impact this fleeting, one-off event had on my life. You see, when I was a little girl, my father (most undoubtedly an undiagnosed Aspie) had a drinking problem and he would beat my mother. He was unpredictable and snaky towards everyone when he was drinking. So I got used to loving men who didn't treat me very well, who were inconsistent, unpredictable…mean and cruel. I had no other father figures in my life to counteract this, except my uncle Howard, who was probably the only man in my life who ever loved me, was kind, and wanted nothing at all from me. I used to love standing on his shiny shoes, while he was wearing them, and wrestling with him. When I was five my father was taken away by police and I never saw him again, until his funeral (when I was nineteen). My beloved uncle died just a couple years later, from a disease that he may have contracted in the Korean War, which caused his organs to fail.

Shortly after Dad left, my mom had a new man in her life. When I was about seven or eight years old, he visited Mom. Alone in the living room with him, I remember I was excited to have a man in the house again so I started to wrestle with him the way I used to do with Dad and Howard. He grabbed my wrists with one hand, grinned at me, and slid his other hand along my crotch and then quickly touched my shirt where my nipples were. I moved away from him feeling sickened and ashamed. This man soon moved in with his many sons, eventually married my mother, and never treated me or my sisters with anything less than contempt. I won't go into our long and horrid history, but I will confess that I have never had what could be called a good relationship, even though I have written books on the subject that work for others (I have the "thank you" mail to prove it). Every man I've been with was either cruel and unpredictable or an alcoholic or both. I had no respect for myself, had no self-esteem whatsoever, until a few months ago, so I never had a chance of having a healthy relationship. Yet.

We are told "honor thy father and mother" and "respect our elders" and are raised to obey authority, in the forms of teachers, police, politicians, etc. The literal mind of the rule-loving Aspie child will be programmed to do this, but we need a caveat: *Some adults do not deserve respect.*

We need to learn the difference between those in positions of power who truly have our interest at heart (e.g. parents), those who are more neutral (e.g. an indifferent teacher) and those who are a threat to our well-being, a menace. Not everyone we dislike is a menace, so there are some subtle and important lessons here where literal children are concerned. It is a *very* serious thing to accuse someone of abuse and I would advise myself and anyone to think carefully and clearly before doing so.

Open communication—use dolls if you have to—to show a child what is not appropriate touching. If you suspect abuse in your child's life, even if you ask them, they may not tell you because of the shame and embarrassment and fear of the adult punishing them. Even at my age, I would not confront certain family members about this, for fear that my eight step-brothers and sisters, their spouses and children—my step-dad's grandchildren—would all accuse me of lying. (Fortunately, they don't read.) So I must hope that justice will be karmically served, and I get on with my life, without him in it. Making this confession to others, including my sister, and shutting my mom and step-dad out of my life allowed me, for the first time in my life, to sleep without nightmares. I can sometimes now go two or three nights without night terrors. This has never happened, since I can remember, since very early childhood.

If you have demons, you have to exorcise them. You do that by talking them out but also by showing them the door. As Glinda the good witch once said, "Begone, you have no power here."

▶ **Shopping** While a full refrigerator and closet is a beautiful thing, shopping is usually not very high on an Aspie's list of favorite things to do. There are lots of reasons for this. Fluorescent lighting, bad pop music, too many items whooshing past our peripheral vision when walking or being pushed in a cart. Deceptive, hard-to-read labels, and too many choices! The cereal aisle is mind-boggling; I'm grateful there are so few gluten-free varieties. High prices, illogical arrangements of goods, grumpy cashiers who grimace when we bring our own environmentally friendly bags, or scowl when we ask them to please put more than two items in each one; the necessity for small talk…all these things make us want to sign on to Amazon.

Really successful food shopping on a budget takes sleuthing, ingenuity, a bit of traveling and, of course, your sensory toolkit. I won't address junk food discipline too much. We do that elsewhere in this book. One rule? If you don't know what an ingredient is, and it sounds like it came out of a test tube, don't buy it. A healthy, balanced, organic or gluten-free diet can be expensive, so one must look out for the sales, or the best places to buy in bulk. Usually a combination of things will be best: grow some produce, and buy locally grown produce from a farm stand or farmers' market; have a mainstay supermarket, whether it's Tesco in England or Wegmans in New York, then possibly a supplemental one, like Aldi or Trader Joe's; lastly, some things will be cheaper, or only available in your area, by purchasing online.

Malls are the new town center for Americans: where they purchase goods but also where they get their exercise, parading up and down and checking out their peers, the smell of overly sweet, oversized cinnamon rolls filling the air. As an Aspie I preferred the cobblestoned pedestrian roads of my small Welsh town, or the train-serviced city centres of Liverpool and York where fresh air off the moors and the Mersey (okay maybe not so fresh) managed to infiltrate the town air with its aromas of meat pies and curry being held close to our noses by the British drizzle. Where you'd dart in and out of the cold, and reward yourself at the end with a nice Sunday roast and a pint or chili and chips. Most Americans will never know what that's like, unless they live in a city with village-like neighborhoods, such as Manhattan, San Francisco, New Orleans and the like.

As much as it is good to support your local economy, buying locally made goods and produce, online outlets are perfect for us and can at least pick up the slack. If you're worried about what that's doing to your local economy, you can easily search if the goods are made in your own country, which means more jobs at home.

For clothes and furniture try visiting small independent stores, especially vintage boutiques and antique shops, because frankly, these things were made much better in the past. At any rate, we must fight the corporate takeover of absolutely everything! I swear they'll put a Walmart in space if we ever see signs of life out there.

Buying clothes I use the Braille method and choose clothing first by feel. (For a long time, I headed straight for the pajama department, because nothing else was comfortable enough.) Oh yes, it needs to catch the eye, but do look away while you feel the fabric. If it gives even the slightest uncomfortable sensation let it go. If it passes the touch test, look at it. What does the color/pattern say? Does it sing to you, call out "Take me home," or does it confuse or even repel? If the experience is positive move on to the next phase: is it practical, meaning does it fit with your lifestyle? Do you actually have a use for it other than ego-based? (Actually now that I think about it, the same criteria could apply to my next boyfriend.) Lastly, try it on. Is it comfortable? Life's too short to be itched and pinched. Does it look good? Some of us tend to be a bit frumpy in our clothing choices, because comfort is key. Unless you live in a cabin in the woods, you shouldn't look like you do.

Last word on shopping: it can be the single person's substitute for sex and contact. The amount of money you spend may be commensurate with how frustrated you are. It can also be an expensive antidote to boredom. Know your motivation.

▶ **Sleep issues** (see *Nightmares*) Sleep is something that many people take for granted; it comes at the end of the day, sure as sundown. Undoubtedly one of the simple pleasures in life. For others, it is not so simple.

Many people, on and off the spectrum, have trouble falling and/or staying asleep. This can be caused by a number of factors. Caffeine, sugar, drugs, chemicals, sensory or social overstimulation, worries and cares, a loud environment, too much light (streetlamps, seasonal sun), wrong pajamas, wrong blankets, temperature, the list goes on. Approaching this challenge scientifically and not reacting emotionally will help. For example, if you drink coffee and someone suggests you cut down, rushing to the defensive is not going to solve the problem. Systematic experimentation will be key. There are dozens if not hundreds of tips for good sleep. Here are just a few:

- Relax for a while before bed to help you wind down towards sleep. I don't know too many people on the spectrum who can just walk in the door, throw themselves down and immediately head to slumber land.

- Earplugs.

- Very soft sheets.

- Blackout curtains.

- Chamomile tea before bed.

- Weighted blankets.

- Massage (you can do your own face/pressure point massage).

- Sleep mask.

- Lavender sachets or oils.

- Leave the TV on all night, or, keep it off. Experiment to see which you like better.

- Get some fresh air and exercise every day.

- Hot bath a few hours before bed.

- Yoga before bed.

- Nature sounds.

- Bergamot oil (found in Earl Grey tea which has caffeine, but if drunk in the afternoon can help you at night).

- Eat turkey (it contains tryptophan which makes one sleepy).

- Melatonin will not help autistics stay asleep but may help you fall asleep. Do not take too much as it will work as a depressant.

- Drugs, over the counter or prescription. These are never high on my list; you have to sleep every night for the rest of your life, so getting dependent on a pharmaceutical to allow you to do this most natural of things is not recommended. However, it may help on occasion or even "teach" your body how to sleep, so for a short time may be okay.

- I swear by a shot of vodka. Every evening, I have a vodka martini and after the drink is done, I usually sleep like a baby with no other aids ingested other than chamomile. Obviously, if you are underage, an alcoholic or teetotaler, please ignore this suggestion.

The body needs to rest and rejuvenate, so if you are sleep-deprived, I'd suggest you make it a special area of study until you've mastered it at least a little bit. You may find several tricks not on this list.

▶ **Smiling** (see *Negativity*) As part of our social training as new little people on this planet, we may be told that people will find us more approachable if we smile…and it's usually true. But although our intent may be to open doors and make friends, we can't always be certain that someone smiling at us has the same intent.

Literal, innocent Aspies be warned: you cannot always tell when someone is genuinely nice just because they're smiling and *acting* nice. They might be smiling because they just did something horrible to someone, they might be smiling because they just got something they wanted. They might smile because they know they look more attractive when they do.

Some people smile simply because they want people to like them. To Aspies that may seem like a form of social bribery. However, smiling does help others feel at ease around you. In brief, formal or light-hearted social situations, keeping one's true feelings under wraps is often necessary, otherwise every encounter with a cashier or barista could turn into a lengthy or inappropriately personal conversation. Sometimes it's best to just smile and say, "Thank you, have a nice day."

Polite smiles can turn into genuine smiles of warmth as you get to know someone. Genuine smiles of happiness and satisfaction will also come with self-acceptance, awareness and learning to celebrate achievements, however big or small.

▶ **Social imagination** (see *Theory of mind*) Social imagination helps us to understand and even predict the behavior of other people; to imagine situations outside our immediate daily routine. This is challenging to people on the spectrum and is part of the criteria for diagnosis.

▶ **Social media (SM)** Every minority needs a homeland, every subculture a mother ship. Republicans have Fox News, senior citizens have casinos, Aspies have Facebook.

The internet is made for us, and we know this, yet we may take criticism for using social media exactly as it's intended: for socializing. While some of us do spend far too much time on SM, I can't help but think there may be an element of envy; just as we might envy a non-autistic who has a lot of friends and moves with ease through a social situation, someone might envy us our popularity online. It's our medium of choice because we are a community that is spread across the globe and many of us don't have anyone IRL that gets us. We also tend to communicate far better in writing than in non-scripted speech, so we have taken to Facebook like eagles to the air.

A couple of warnings:

- *Posting on Facebook when one is troubled may be seen as seeking a pity-party* rather than a reaching out. We do better on the page, while NAs fare better in the real world. While they may have spent their week out and about, talking about life and its challenges with friends, an Aspie may have been completely alone, with only their online friends to talk to. Why is one more valid than the other? It isn't, but sometimes our personal problems should be kept private, away from prying, spying eyes that may not have our best interests at heart.

- *No matter what, don't name names online if you're hurt or upset at someone.* No matter how much they deserve it, things will be taken out of context and you will look like the baddie. I've done it once or twice and I'm still regretting it.

- *If you say anything remotely controversial it may be misread or misinterpreted.* It's very rare for people to read posts accurately. They will impute different things into it, interpret based on their own experience, or rush to comment without reading all the way through. Sometimes they also don't read others' comments and so they say the same thing a hundred other people did.

- *You can't really tell what people are like online.* Some people I've met in person whom I didn't like online turned out to be lovely. Others have seemed really cool online but when I met them they were not at all what I had anticipated. Other people who were ardent followers and flatterers, always tagging me in things, commenting on my every post, turned out to be trouble, sometimes big trouble. (Ever see the movie *All About Eve*?) You just can't always tell. Try to give people the benefit of the doubt, but don't be too quick to trust.

- *Do not feel bad if, like me, you do not participate in online groups.* It is nice to have a community online to talk to, but I have heard of very nasty experiences in online Aspie groups. In-fighting, gossip and bitchiness.

- *Never add people to groups without asking*—it feels like a hijacking.

- *Don't be one of these people who creates a page or an account every time they think a semi-interesting thought.* Once you create one of these things, it's hard to get rid of. Facebook and other social media sites will hang onto you like a hungry zombie. And never create a page for someone without asking. Someone did that for me and I nearly died of embarrassment. She wanted people to send money because I was going through a difficult time, bless her heart. Luckily she put me on as an admin so I was able to deactivate the page, but not before the gossips caught wind of it and accused me of creating it myself.

- Back in the 1970s, "Man I dig your crazy threads" meant you liked someone's clothes, not their bizarre FB posts. Posting strange and eccentric things will show your true colors. *If you plan on having a lot of professional colleagues visiting your page, you might want a separate one* for your UFO conspiracy buddies.

- *Never post anything BC or AD*: before coffee or after a drink.

- *What is with poking?* Never poke me online or in real life. I will punch you.

- *Don't say mean things or make negative comments unless absolutely necessary.* If someone says something you disagree with, or a joke you don't understand, it's best to move on and find something you *do* like or understand. If you must question someone, perhaps because it's an important topic and you feel you can enlighten or contribute, do so with respect, and better yet, do it in a private message. When you post on someone's page, it is like walking into their house and making a comment. The same amount of tact should apply. You wouldn't walk into someone's living room and say, "I hate your couch." There are people who only comment negatively; I can't stand those cowardly keyboard warriors.

- *If someone comes into your "living room" and acts like a brat, you have every right to show them the door and lock them out.* There's a difference between friendly disagreement and some stranger just showing up on your page saying they don't like something you've said and then stirring up a big rabble against you. That happens far too often, and Aspies are as guilty as anyone. You have every right to block someone who is being inappropriate.

- *Sending people unsolicited advice in a message, or psychic predictions about their life, is the height of impertinence.* If we want guidance, we each have our friends who we turn to, counselors or books. There are the pedantic types on SM who can't resist showing up in people's inboxes spouting "you should" and "you ought to."

- *One more word of caution about the internet:* Last year a school got busted for spying on kids with laptops that they sent home with their students. Remember when webcams used to have lights so you knew when they were on? They no longer do that (thank you NSA, Bush and the so-called *Patriot Act*). You never know who's looking. So keep it legal and moral. And to be safe, put a piece of tape over the camera so no one can see you pick your nose.

  We are all being spied on now. By the government, but also by search engines. And they are each only getting snapshots of us. As a result Facebook thinks I live in San Francisco, Netflix thinks I'm a gay British male, and Canadian online pharmacies think I need Viagra. Now, if I were a gay British male living in San Francisco, I'd like to think I wouldn't need Viagra, thank you very much.

▶ **Socializing IRL (in real life)** As much as I get so many of my needs met online, I don't get them all met. As I said above, most of us on the spectrum do like to socialize from time to time, in an interesting way, with interesting or kind people, especially at Aspie-friendly events. Here are a few examples of events, places and groups that one might be involved with on a frequent or infrequent basis: Comic Con, church, theatre, choir, band, meditation, gigs and concerts, trekking (both earth and star varieties), bird-watching, exercise, writing, gaming (IRL), knitting, drum circles, volunteering, reenactment, environmental, cosplay, Asperger's. There's probably a million more. Try Meetup[36] to start the ball rolling.

Some of us don't get much socializing beyond chitchat with our local shopkeepers and we may be shy even of that. But small-talking with strangers can actually be good practice for neutral, unemotional exchanges. You probably don't have a tangled history with your local grocer, so a little "Hi, how are you?" can be very nice. And the time constraints of a passing exchange limit the possibility of social faux pas. But don't assume someone you've had a chat with, even several times, considers himself your friend. Most people do take a long time, even years, to get to that point with someone.

The longer I live, the more I realize that the only time I feel truly comfortable socializing is when I'm in a place where Aspies are the majority. Nothing against non-Aspies, but I find it tiring trying to figure out what they're about to say and if I committed some transgression according to their own subcultural mores. It is difficult to be a minority all the time, having to walk and talk like the natives. So, I prefer the company of nice, non-judgmental people, and usually for me, those turn out to be Aspies, fellow geeks and oddballs.

Having said that, there will be many, many times in your life that you will be swimming in a sea of non-autistics. When that happens, try to find the things we have in common and make new friends.

If you are newly diagnosed, you may want to tell everyone you meet, but there's a time and a place. If your announcement is out of context or a non-sequitur (see *Disclosure*) it will do more harm than good for your cause.

If you are lonely and depressed, and inertia sets in, it can be very difficult to climb back up that muddy embankment. Prevent it by scheduling regular social time, even if it's just once a week or twice a month, whether it's with a family member or a friend. I once saw a news report where young Japanese couples "rented" old people to visit on Sundays if their own were too far away, to give them that family feeling. While *rent-a-gran* is never going to take off in the west, you can still visit a local nursing home, bring cards and flowers, and play a tune on the piano.

We should and often do find other Aspies to connect with starting from a young age, but sometimes the "weird kids" will reject each other for fear of being seen as even more weird and will instead want to mix with the cool kids for validation, especially if we are filled with self-loathing and wish we could be totally different. Some thoughts on this: Yes, we all want to be seen as cool. If you don't want to be in the science club and sit at the revenge of the nerds table at lunch, at least be kind to your Aspie cousins and recognize they are, in many ways, your people. You will also find spectrum folks in rock bands and other "cooler" places but at the end of the day, rock star or not, you're still an Aspie and to some extent, my friend, a geek. Be proud of it. Many geeks reach great heights and redefine coolness in film, music, arts and sciences.

Socializing will never be easy for us, but the rewards can be great. According to Tony Attwood, for every hour of socializing, you will need up to an hour of downtime. You will find you are overstimulated when you leave a social situation. Much of it will replay in your head. Have a *healthy* way to come back down, to decompress. If for every hour of socializing you need an hour of alcohol, or chocolate, those are not great coping skills. I sometimes feel disappointed or confused when I leave social situations. I wonder if I said the wrong thing, or if I misinterpreted others' behavior in the moment. Staying sober and mindful, being healthy and relaxed (as much as possible), employing the tips we've been given here, will help minimize the anxiety and maximize the joy that can come from connecting with others.

I've heard it said that it is only in the mirror of another's eyes that you can truly see yourself becoming complete. I don't think I believe this, but I do think it is *part* of the process of maturity and becoming you.

▶ **Someday** is what procrastinators say. If you won't do it now, what makes you think you'll do it someday?

▶ **Soothing behaviors** (aka stimming) Rocking, flapping, flicking, clapping, picking, whirling, clicking, twirling, spinning, singing, squealing and flinging, oh, it's all such good fun.

I asked a roomful of teachers and admin at an autism lecture, "What am I doing?" as I rocked from side to side on my feet.

"Self-stimulating!" they shouted in unison.

"I am not, nor would I wish to be, stimulated at this time, thank you," I replied.

"Self-regulating!" they tried again.

"I beg your pardon. I am not a Swiss watch. I am merely soothing myself because I am nervous."

The group went on to say that their students do things like that when they are bored and tired. That is another function of rocking, but in my experience of interviewing many people on the spectrum, stims tend to be a release of nervousness and anxiety; a way to *soothe*. All the big fancy words just make things seem way more complicated than they need to be.

A mother came to me and said, "My daughter rocks in class and I'm trying to get her to stop."

"Why?" I asked. "Is it for her benefit, yours, the teachers, the other students? Why is she rocking, what will you give her to replace it?"

If our need to soothe is suppressed, where is that anxiety going to go? You just can't shout at us to stop. It may take the form of ulcers, in an already vulnerable digestive system. It may take the form of self-destructive habits like hair-pulling, self-immolation, bulimia, or negative thinking that goes on infinite repeat. Some of these things can become an OCD and very debilitating.

The motto is: replace don't repress. Kicking the chair in front of you? Try taking up kickboxing. Humming all the time? Join a choir. You see where I'm going with this. Try to find positive or at least less intrusive replacements for soothing behaviors that may be disruptive to oneself and others.

A sensory room is not a luxury perk, it is beneficial to everyone, and a sensory toolkit is crucial. There will be things in there that alleviate anxiety. As I mentioned in *Medication*, an adult can make their own informed choices, but giving mind-altering drugs to a child is *very* serious business. One had better exhaust all other possibilities before taking such a route. Try asking what's bothering them, for starters. They may tell you and it may surprise you. It could be anything from boredom with the material, a dislike of the teacher, fluorescent lights, to being disliked, to very serious bullying. A pill isn't going to fix any of that. Most likely diet will play a massive role in a child's capacity to concentrate and their sensory discomfort threshold.

▶ **Speech delay** (see *Echophenomena*, *Selective mutism*) There's an old joke. A couple and their seven-year-old autistic son are at the dinner table. The boy has never spoken. Suddenly out of nowhere he says, "These potatoes are cold." The parents are overjoyed. "Why have you never spoken before?" they ask. "Because up to now, everything's been fine," answers the boy. I don't mean to make light, but you simply cannot tell what a person is thinking by their lack of speech. We all know that Temple Grandin and other well-known geniuses on the spectrum were considered to be mentally deficient as children, and look how they turned out. Temple is one of the most eloquent and humorous speakers I've ever heard.

Have you ever had laryngitis to the point where you could not speak? Did your brain cease to function? Did your IQ drop? Probably not. A person who is not yet speaking, what I call *preverbal* as opposed to nonverbal (let's be realistic, most people with autism do talk eventually), is still a thinking individual. The silent child at the dinner table might be waiting for something to say, a chance to jump on the carousel. He or she might feel that they have nothing to contribute. Maybe the conversation has yet to touch on something that interests them. They may be overwhelmed with sensory stimulation that has them lost in a world of their own. Perhaps they are very happy being in their thoughts. It may be so peaceful in there, why leave the mind palace for the unpredictable streets of the human race?

One cannot always tell the cause, but as a parent, you will want to do your best to encourage communication, to know your child and to be sure that they are not trapped in a world of discomfort. If you or your child have difficulty communicating, there are tools, apps and devices that can speak aloud for you. There are also therapies (behavioral, speech, music, etc.) which use a variety of approaches. If a person has occasional bouts of inability to speak that is usually called selective mutism and is different from delayed speech.

▶ **Sports** I have heard it said that playing team sports is great for people on the spectrum for a few reasons. It helps with proprioception and hand–eye coordination. It also makes you a team member, so as long as you play decently you'll have comrades, something we may be otherwise lacking.

Aspies can and do become great athletes, even to the Olympic level. Most of us will enjoy solitary sports like swimming and gymnastics and those will at least help with coordination and health issues. Others will simply enjoy non-competitive exercises of the mind–body variety.

Many of us will think that the obsessive sport-watching of a large percentage of the world is nothing short of bizarre, as valid a mental health disorder as any in the DSM. We understand the fun of playing ball, but getting emotionally invested in the outcome of a game played by millionaires who were bought to represent your city? Truly illogical, Captain. Some people get very depressed when their team loses and jubilant when they win. It is a risky thing to invest your emotions in something so arbitrary, but if you truly enjoy it, no harm done I suppose. Those of us who don't understand the appeal must try not to judge others or begrudge their enjoyment. You can shake your head and quote Julius Caesar, shouting, "Bread and circuses," but look where being pompous got him.

▶ **Step-parenting** I feel this is a subject not discussed often enough but with families being much more fluid than they once were, it's an important one. A child of a single parent is usually completely powerless to influence any outcome of that parent's dating choices, and really has to hope for the best that they will choose someone suitable for them. This is perhaps even more important where a spectrum child is concerned. We may have been traumatized by the removal or departure of one parent from the scene, for even if they made the remaining parent unhappy, they may not have affected the child in this way. Even unhappiness that you're used to can be difficult for an Aspie kid to adjust to living without. So let's say the child has adjusted, and now here comes a new "parent" on the scene. They may have absolutely no idea what Asperger's is about, and they may look at the child's sensory, social and cognitive differences as misbehaving, attention-seeking and other negative things.

Whether there is anyone on the spectrum or not, I firmly believe that a step-mum or dad must be fully aware of the responsibilities of taking on a child, and be willing to be an authentic parent to them, even if the other parent is still in the picture. Too often people use "I'm not his *real* dad" as an excuse to make little effort in the child's life. Whether this is born of apathy or not wanting to make mistakes with a child who isn't genetically your own, this can be seriously damaging. If you bring someone into an Aspie child's life, you had all better be ready to be the support group that the kid needs, or there will be damage to the psyche and to self-esteem which can be lifelong.

This also applies to people on the spectrum who become step-parents. You must be the kind of parent you would have wanted yourself, and not let your tendency to close off or self-isolate keep you from developing an affectionate and loving relationship with your step-kids. When Aunt Aspie was a little girl, Dad was taken out of the picture and she was left with four (mostly) NT siblings and a mom who was only concerned about finding a man who made *her* happy. Once Mr. Neanderthal moved in with his little cave-dwellers, my traits, even my positive ones like hyperlexia and good grades, instead of being praised, were ignored and even ridiculed. Almost up to this very day, my love of reading was deemed a waste of time, my accomplishments, flukes.

If you are a single parent looking for love I would advise finding someone who sees the good in you and your children and who realizes that you are a package deal. They should bolster the confidence of the child instead of tearing down everything about them. Ignoring your children should not be an option for them. If you marry for yourself, knowing that the person and your child are not compatible, I caution that you may end up with a sticky mess on your hands, and guilt, eventually, may be your constant companion. I'd suggest thinking it through and, if possible, at least waiting until the child has grown to a less vulnerable age.

▶ **Stimming** (see *Soothing behaviors*)

▶ **Strengths, abilities and challenges** Every person in the world has strengths and deficits. In the case of the Aspie the deficits may be in areas that surprise, e.g. common sense. There's a line in *London Boulevard* where Harry (played by Colin Farrell) says to eccentric, reclusive and gifted actress Charlotte, "What you are is not what everybody is. It's alright to have trouble with the basics. It would be odd if you didn't."

Now, if each of us only had our own personal Colin Farrell to say that to us. (Oy, he does make Auntie hot under her apron!) Every person on the spectrum is going to have strengths in one or more areas, and many of us will take those to a proficient level. Some of us will take one or two things to a prodigious level. And every one of us is going to have one or more areas in which we struggle: things which may be easy for others, such as socializing, small-talking, driving, etc.

You've heard it before but I'll say it again: know your strengths but work on your challenges, especially if they are in an area that is important to you. Do what you can to improve, not to "pretend to be normal" (thank you, Liane Holliday Willey), but to make your life better, to please yourself. As Tony Attwood says, "It's better to be a first-rate Aspie than a second-rate NT."

Acknowledge and celebrate your progress, even if it's at a modest pace. If you do have some promising abilities, no matter in what field (as long as it's legal), work on them because that's where your purpose most likely is, and without purpose, we on the spectrum flounder.

▶ **Stress and panic attacks** (see *Anxiety*) Everyone has stress. Like self-love, in small amounts it is healthy. If you had no stress, you'd never find out what you were capable of, what your mettle looked like. When stress is chronic and more than we can and should be able to manage, then it becomes dangerous. Tax season, divorce, moving house, changing jobs, birth, death, marriage, bullying, some of us have so many events happening all the time that our pulse never seems to slow down to a healthy rate. Signs of too much stress include heart palpitations, chest pains, stomach pains and other digestion problems, depression, dizziness, nightmares, lethargy, headaches and more.

How you cope with stress will be a big factor in how your body holds up. Do you binge eat, and drink copious amounts of pop or alcohol? Or do you hit the mat, trail or gym? (See *Diet*, *Exercise*.)

Panic attacks happen when the signs and symptoms of too much stress hit you all at once and are so powerful you may think you are experiencing a heart attack or other critical physical event. A person who has a panic attack for the first time may think they are dying and dial for emergency help. While your demise is probably not imminent, it *is* a big wake-up call that something is not right in your world. Prolonged stress *can* kill you in the form of heart attacks, strokes and more.

I never had panic attacks when I lived in the UK, because I knew that my basics would always be provided for if I needed them. In the US, where it is much more "survival of the fittest," I have them frequently, as there are far fewer safety nets preventing a person losing their home and other material goods (not to mention their teeth). Perhaps I'm being nostalgic, but it seems that when Auntie was a girl no one ever heard of panic attacks. But life was truly much more simple then in many ways, even in the States. Fewer rules, less expensive, less surveillance, less serious violence, less religious fanaticism. I'm not saying it was perfect—indeed, things have improved in many ways for many people. I'm simply saying there was less of a feeling of impending doom. Global problems such as fighting over natural resources and climate change were still decades into the future, etc. Now, there's a whole lot of stuff dropped into our laps every day. Sometimes, when it comes to stressors, we have to face them head on and deal with them. Other times, we just need to go outside, take off our shoes and wiggle our toes in the grass.

There are countless ways to alleviate stress, from taking the day off, turning off the news(!), going to the beach or forest, engaging in physical exercise, having sex, watching a comedy. One of my favorites is bird-watching, although I do it passively from my desk. (Bird-watching talk is either surreal or dirty-sounding. If I don't have a cardinal in my shrubbery, I have a tufted titmouse on my feeder or a hawk in my bush. Don't even get me started on the woodpecker.) Do something about your stress levels, or they may eventually do something about you.

▶ **Substance abuse** This requires much more attention than we can possibly give it here, but we'll do our best to address the issue. On the one hand, we are told substance abuse is bad. On the other hand, we are bombarded from every direction with drugs and alcohol, legal, sanctioned, illegal, illicit, from doctors, in our neighborhoods, in films and on television. It is difficult to be moderate when there's just so much of it about, particularly if you are genetically prone to addictive behavior, and/or you live with those who are (many spouses of alcoholics end up becoming alcoholics for example), or you go through some horrendous experience in your life that is almost unbearable and so you choose to chemically escape.

You will receive no judgment from Auntie. But you will, of course, get her two cents. I personally feel there is nothing wrong with a nightcap or a glass of wine with dinner or the occasional spliff if it is legal in your area and you are an adult with a fully formed brain. I think that if you have exhausted all possibilities and the only thing that gets you through your life is the little blue pill the doctor gives you, it "ain't nobody's business if you do." However, if you live to drink/smoke/toke/medicate, then something is wrong with this picture. There are so many things we could be doing with our lives. Many of us feel helpless and hopeless, and inertia sets in. We live in the culturally barren suburbs, disconnected from the earth, from each other, from spirit. The TV sits there, beckoning, as do all the substances. There you sit, bored and/or stressed, and medicate.

Make no mistake about it. You are not abusing substances, you are abusing YOU. When Auntie lived with one beau she found out he was what some call a *juice hound*. All the nagging in the world couldn't get him to cut down on the booze, so she joined him. She drank and drank and laughed and partied, and got a bit paunchy in the middle, a bit saggy in the jowls, and a bit loose in the lips. She lost many friends and professional contacts because of her raucous behavior. Now maybe Uncle NT can be a jolly drinker, but Aspies tend to say the unexpected to begin with; add alcohol and stir, and some serious transgressions can be made. Add domestic spats and AS meltdowns to the mix and it's amazing nobody ended up in jail.

In addition to the drink, Auntie also decided to finally get a good night's sleep so she began taking some heavy-duty pharmaceuticals that she got Uncle to get for her from his doctor. It is a miracle that she's still here. Uncle lost a relative to substance abuse and suicide. Six months later, Auntie and Uncle broke up. Shortly after that, Auntie lost a sister to substance abuse and accidental suicide. That was a massive wake-up call. The pills went down the toilet, the wine cellar was converted and re-purposed, and sobriety became the norm.

Auntie still likes a drink. But on the rare occasion of one too many, she is swiftly reminded that there is a fine line between having a drink, and the drink having her.

Some people with addictive personalities are all or nothing and they will never be able to have just one. Everyone is different. We cannot all paint with the same brush. Know who you are, know your limitations, and don't be afraid to admit when you need real help. When you finally stop abusing yourself, it's amazing how much more time you will have, how much more energy to do the things you've always wanted to do. The sky's the limit.

▶ **Suicide/suicidal thoughts** When you hit rock bottom you have two choices, either get up or go under…six feet under. You can't stay on the bottom, it's far too excruciating a state. And it is not human nature to remain static. After a while you begin to stir, make a cup of tea, eat something, look out the window. Thoughts creep in…what to do now, next, tomorrow? We can survive the most horrendous events and conditions, maybe because we are so much stronger than we realize.

We may have a go at suicide—a practice run, where we put a rope around our neck or take a bottle of something that we know probably won't kill us—to send a message to those we love and who supposedly love us, that we are in a bad way. Maybe we end up in the emergency room, where very likely they will require we spend at least a few days in a mental hospital/psych ward (you will not get politically correct terms from me) for a few nights, but what good will that do? They'll stick you in front of a TV with some sugary drink made of chemicals, and if you're lucky they might numb you with meds for a while. Your ward mates will be the demented and infirm; alcoholics, substance abusers; the lost, lonely and brokenhearted for the most part. The smell of ennui and despair fills the air. Many people will pretend to be worse than they are so that they can continue to get their meds. I know all this because I have personally been in a psychiatric institution after a suicide attempt. This happened after my second husband did a runner and left me and my daughter alone in a foreign country with no money (I was a struggling artist) and an eviction notice from his mother, back in the year 2000.

Attempts at or threats of suicide don't really mean a person wants to die; they want to live and be loved and understood. They want to be heard and appreciated. If they are sick, they want to be well. They no longer want to be in pain. With each repeated attempt, however, they are probably getting more serious about it. That doesn't mean that if they succeed, they won't regret it at the last minute. I've heard stories of people who jumped off a bridge and on the way down changed their minds. They were the ones who lived to tell the tale but what of the ones who didn't? Chances are a great many of them regretted it too.

We've already talked about depression—possible causes, what to do about it. Obviously if you are contemplating suicide either something terribly horrendous has just happened to you, or a steady stream of bad events are chipping away at your will to live. Either way, you have my heartfelt empathy. I have been there. So what do we do about it? Do we hope and pray that our partner/parent/adult child/friend/ boss will change and suddenly see us for the wondrous being that we are? Or do we do something for ourselves, celebrate our own virtues and tenacity?

If you are doing things like substance or alcohol abuse, then address that. Now. Ditto if you are doing some things— perhaps engaging in crime or other activities—which go against your moral code. If you have been caught, you may have to go through some punishment. It's called karma and no one escapes its jaws forever. You will come out the other side.

If you are living well and being the best person you can be and are still getting no joy, then what? Why should you be depressed? So much depression comes from trying to make others love us. Some people never will, or need to go through their own stuff to get to a place where they will. Meanwhile, what can you do? Reach out to people who might get it. I reached out to my Facebook friends about a very personal matter, because I knew that they would get it. We've been friends for years, and we've been there for each other. And since most of them are Aspies, and have been there themselves, they gave me empathy and useful advice, or anecdotes about similar drama in their own lives. However, there were people listening in and judging. If you have a thousand friends, and only a hundred of them communicate with you, it doesn't mean the others aren't spying. So, although it got me through a dark time, I wouldn't do it again because of the judgment and gossip that ensued.

You can't, and probably shouldn't, stay on your computer forever. Power down before you get overwhelmed. Next, take a few days to heal. Don't underestimate the physical toll and exhaustion that being on the threshold of suicide has taken on your body. You probably ache all over, have headaches, are dizzy, can't concentrate, maybe have nausea or other digestion problems. So keep it simple. Eat, drink, bathe, dress, rest. That might be enough for Day One. If you're a teen tell your parents that you are in a very bad state and that you need their love, help and conversation to get you through it. Take a day or two off of school or work. Maybe you have a counselor or friend who is wonderful to talk to. Allow yourself some marathon telly watching, although I'd advise something constructive, like a documentary or perhaps a comedy or period piece as opposed to *Hostel V*, which is only going to add to the darkness in your home. (I love horror films, just not when I'm already living in one.) By Day Two, you can probably incorporate some exercise, even if it's just walking around your garden. By Day Three (or so), back to business as usual but at a gentler pace. Monitor your thoughts and words, to see if you're feeding your depression and taking yourself back to square one. You may have done something embarrassing while in the throes of woes. Don't beat yourself up for it. People don't like to see us hit ourselves in the head or cry like babies, but it happens to the best of us. Forgive yourself and move on. I'm not going to say something pithy like time heals all wounds. It doesn't. Some wounds change us forever. The question is, how can you use it to your advantage or to help others?

I'll leave you with this thought. If you are prone to suicidal thinking, never forget this: if you kill yourself, the bastards win.

▶ **Surprises** People on the spectrum generally don't like surprises. From birthday presents to visitors, we prefer to know what's coming than to have something sprung on us. With regard to presents, we like to know what we're getting to ensure that we get what we want, and that you don't waste your time and money on something we don't. It may seem like ingratitude when we turn up our nose at your gift, but it is just practicality.

You may take the day off from work to surprise us with a long weekend at a cabin somewhere and immediately we'll launch into a thousand concerns about weather, wildlife, sleeping quarters, food, etc., making the office seem much more appealing than it had. This is because we will be wrenched from our ritual and routine and all the things we have arranged to eat, wear, drink and do with our days.

Don't even think about turning up at our home as a surprise visit. If I don't know you're coming, you could be Brad Pitt naked on a unicorn and I'd still scream, "Get off my property you varmint" like a deranged younger version of Granny from *The Beverly Hillbillies*. Surprises frighten us, none more than someone invading our sanctuary unannounced. Prosopagnosia may play a role. We may not immediately recognize the person walking up our path, or their car, for prosopagnosia can also extend to vehicle recognition. Our brain computers will be scanning the scene, trying to make sense of it. An unrecognized visitor, for some of us, is terrifying. I once screamed at a duo of Jehovah's Witnesses who'd sat in a car in front of my house for several minutes with two others before they all got out and headed to various doors. It made me so nervous that by the time I'd figured out what they were, it was too late. I could only yell, "Go away, I'm good with God!" From the way I shrieked it I probably seemed much more aligned with the other guy.

This aversion to surprises can be a mood-killer and make people want to stop doing things for us, especially at holidays. If you are on the spectrum, try to learn to like them (and I know some of you already do). You can practice in small ways. If, for example, your partner asks what you want for dinner, say, "Surprise me." And then don't proceed to criticize or cook another course. Enjoy the fact that someone has done something for you, freeing you up. When it comes to vacations, a lot will be out of your control. You will survive it and it will make coming home all the more satisfying. At the end of the day, none of us has total control over our lives, our environments, even the moment of our death. I hate to play Freud here, but I think our fear of surprises actually has something to do with fear of that ultimate surprise.

▶ **Swearing** (see *Profanity*)

T

▶ **Tact and diplomacy** are not dirty words relegated to cheesy politicians. These are the tools of a successful social life. Tact is the antidote to bluntness. Shooting a verbal arrow may be the fastest way to get your point across, but targets may step aside and try to avoid you in future. We all like words that open doors and make us feel engaged as opposed to coerced, criticized or controlled. You could be the wisest, kindest person in the world, but if you don't learn the art of tact, you will build an invisible wall around yourself a hundred feet thick.

Like when giving advice, being tactful requires stepping back for a moment and finding the most constructive way to say something, or whether to say it at all. It can actually be quite pleasurable and give us a much better feeling inside than the almost imperceptible judder we may feel when we are tactless, but don't know exactly what we said wrong. We can make tact a special course of study, invaluable in expanding our social horizons. Look for the positive, speak the positive and you will almost certainly expand your circle of friends.

▶ **Talent** Most people on the spectrum are talented in some area. If we find that we have a natural aptitude for something, we can become exceptionally talented at it through application and diligence. While few of us are at the level of a savant, many people on the spectrum do become musicians, artists and writers of note. In addition to natural talent and obsessive focus, our higher fluid intelligence may also play a role—putting things together in new ways, drawing lines connecting things that may not have been connected before but which we see clearly.

I've already mentioned that the creative side of autism is often overlooked by job counselors and the like. Part of this is the underestimation of the importance of the arts in society, and also in our lives, personally. It may also be due to the fact that we may not present the stereotypical image of an artist: cool, savvy, socially popular.

In addition to innate talent I think we cultivate performing art skills for a purpose. In *Aspergirls*[37] I wrote about how the adrenalin that others trigger in us can cause us to either shut down or over-perform and how we may have difficulty finding a middle ground. I think there's another aspect to that too. Because so many of us are ignored in real life, underestimated, we *choose* to perform—write, act, sing, play—to create a place where we can get attention in a positive way, where there's a script. This is our controlling side, sure, but that would be an oversimplification. It is not attention-seeking for attention's sake, but a way to show people our good side so they'll like us.

All my life I used singing as a way to be attractive to NAs, but I see now that I wasted my time. Even if liked on stage, off stage my unusual and awkward manner pushed most people away. When people think you're weird, being talented can provoke the "I'm surprised you can do that" reaction, which can even take the form of anger and jealousy. We attract naysayers and people may be stunned when we show them what we can do; remember the judges' reactions to Susan Boyle? It is possible that non-autistics have as difficult a time reading us as we do them, and that upsets them, freaks them out a little.

Many of us are renaissance artists (meaning that we excel at many things, not that we paint like Michelangelo). That too can provoke jealousy and even refusal to acknowledge our different facets. To be pigeonholed is as hurtful to us as it would be to anyone.

Create art for art's sake and because you enjoy it, never to get in with the cool kids. And certainly not for fame or money. But if you can find a way to make a living through your art, go for it. A hundred dollars earned doing what you love is worth a thousand doing what you don't.

▶ **Television** If aliens landed like in a 1950s' film and said, "Take us to your leader," we'd have to march them straight to our living rooms and plonk their shiny behinds in front of the telly. This is the real leader, the great brain in our society, that tells us what to think, how to act, what to do. We follow it like sheep, worship those who are on it. I'll say little on this subject except, at least in the US, *kill your cable*! You do not need 250 channels of garbage, and no one needs five minutes of commercials for every five minutes of whatever you are watching. We should no more allow our brains to be bombarded with bad programs and commercials than we should allow someone to spike our food with chemicals.

▶ **Theory of mind** is the knowledge and realization that other people have different needs, wants, points of view and experiences of their own. (I do realize the irony of including this in such an opinionated book.)

▶ **Transitions** Change is not easy for us. Transitions can be major events; changing schools, moving house, getting a step-parent, starting or ending relationships; or they can be everyday, banal things, like going from a quiet place into a noisy one, going from one activity or class to another.

In order to transition, one has to disengage from one thing, become aware of what is coming next, and then engage in the next thing.

Disengaging. Because a spectrum person usually has to hyperfocus on whatever it is that they're doing, disengaging can be very unpleasant. To you, Junior is just putting away crayons. However, Junior is completely engrossed in his task and invested in its outcome, and for him to pull away at this moment is as annoying and unthinkable as it is for you to leave the cinema five minutes before the climactic ending. Junior is determined to put them away perfectly, in order, and will not be able to put his school clothes on until that task is done.

Becoming aware. Some things make transitions obvious, like a school bell ringing or punching your time card, but other transitions depend on a verbal suggestion or command or even unspoken, nonverbal language. We might not hear or understand subtler signals. Defining transitions can be helpful, such as when you tell a small child that bedtime is at nine o'clock. Adults on the spectrum, too, can find clear delineations liberating.

Adjusting to the new. Extra time is needed to adjust to whatever new circumstance has just come about. Your wife may have just packed for a trip and gotten into your car, a big enough deal in itself. She may not be ready to hear your favorite death metal just yet. There has already been a whirlwind of movement and another sensory onslaught is about to begin—motion, sound, etc.—and it will take a while to get used to *that*.

Shedding. After we disengage, if there is time, there will be a period of shedding the sights, sounds, thoughts, etc. that just came before. You'll find many Aspies like to be early for work, so that they can have a few quiet minutes to adjust to the new environment before all their workmates get there and the hubbub begins. Similarly, you may want to give your Aspie partner a few minutes to themselves when they get home from work, to wrap their head around being home and to shed the replay that's probably going on in their head, containing the day's events. If there isn't time during the day, shedding can happen at the end of the day, which is why it can take some of us hours to fall asleep.

We may be very quick at some things—as a child I could "name that tune" usually by the end of the first note—but that does not extend to transitions. We can learn to lump things together, for example a child can possibly lump all the separate parts of getting ready for school into one massive chore, but arriving at school is going to be a transition regardless.

Those of us who are a bit OCD might find transitions even harder, if we are mentally or physically engaged in that behavior. If our habits are of the invisible variety, e.g. counting in our heads, it will make it difficult for those around us to tell.

Believe it or not, constant change may become the norm for some of us, whether we are traveling carnies, military kids or rock stars. There will still be ritual and routine within that and a normality about change. Indeed, stopping moving, as in Mom and Dad leave the military or we quit the traveling circus, can bring about very difficult emotional circumstances. This is not purely an Aspie thing. Think about the person who has worked for fifty years and then instead of enjoying retirement, falls quickly into depression and lethargy.

There are many tips for making transitions easier for Aspies. Tangible cues are better than verbal or unspoken ones. Allow and respect rituals and routines and don't expect us to "go with the flow." Allow more time for shedding and transitioning than you would a non-autistic. Don't think that because a person's lifestyle is unorthodox they are a free spirit; if they are on the spectrum, chances are they find transitions very difficult. Demystify what's coming with pictures, video or other tangible items. Describe outcome; bring things full circle. When are we going to be back to where we started? In stories, most journeys end with coming home, back to the safe and the known. At the end of the day, that's all anyone really wants.

▶ **Travel** When I first saw *The Wizard of Oz* as a small child I didn't like the ending. Who would want to go back to colorless Kansas when you could stay in a place of dancing scarecrows, flying monkeys and singing lions? The author, Frank L. Baum, would agree since the book did not end that way; Oz was real and Dorothy not only wanted to go back but did many times in subsequent novels. Now that I am older and I have seen Oz, the Emerald City, the enchanted forest and a world full of ghouls and friends, I'm happy to be back in my proverbial Kansas. It may be colorless, but it's home and, of course, isn't colorless at all. I know where my tea and coffee are, have a fridge full of gluten-free loveliness, my Roku (streaming device), laptops, and a recording studio with a picture window that gets a real four-season view, replete with wildlife and a lake. Heaven.

Thanks to the internet we can dip in and out of Oz any time we want. We can give concerts online, talk to friends face to face, hold meetings, all without the aid of a tornado and a flying house.

Real travel is somewhat overrated these days; gone is the glamour, the fun and the expedience which used to be part of the appeal, due in part to fear, security checks, long lines and canceled flights. On top of that, some countries have been virtually ruined by tourism, becoming tacky, dirty, expensive or false. Others have become carbon copies of the US, and still others are decidedly unfriendly to westerners at the moment.

Having said all that, travel is important for many reasons: nothing educates and changes you like travel, in so many areas, such as art, architecture, music, food, lifestyle, dance, sports, politics. One's appreciation and understanding of the varied beauty of our planet deepens, from mountains, hills, plains, forests, jungles, lakes, rivers, streams, to all the wildlife that flourishes and depends on all these natural resources. It increases your understanding of life to see the roots of culture in Europe, Africa, the Far East; how removed we are yet how similar. It's unfathomable to me that so many will never leave their townships, will never venture beyond their small world, except maybe to visit a rather forced mecca like Vegas or one of the Disneys.

There are many motives for travel. Vacation, escape, sporting activities and education mainly, but many undiagnosed spectrumites might travel in search of their people. Never forget that we're everywhere: one in eighty-eight, give or take. You *do* belong, no matter where you are.

Which leads us to the old adage, "Wherever you go, there *you* are." I had the hardest time understanding that from the first time I read it as a child. It made my literal mind bark, "Of course, you ninny, where else would I be?" It's only recently that I really truly understood it. If you aren't getting along with your neighbors now, what makes you think you'll get along with them in Bulgaria?

Some tips for air travel

- When booking a flight, pick the one with the bigger plane; small ones are more likely to be diverted or canceled in bad weather.

- It's better to pay a little more for a flight with fewer or no changeovers, because there's less chance for missed connections and cancellations. If there are cancellations, you almost certainly have to pay for your own hotel, food and transport unless you're a premier member of that airline's frequent flyer program.

- When frightened on a plane, for example during turbulence, find someone more scared than you and comfort them. This will make you both feel better.

- Bring a real book, because at least for now, there are long periods of time when all devices must be turned off. If you end up circling over a city it can go on for an hour or sometimes longer.

- Always pee before you get on any plane or train, and bring snacks. On a plane you can't bring any snacks on board that you didn't buy in the airport itself. So eat before you go and buy a salad in the airport to bring on board where they have mostly really unhealthy things and charge a small fortune for them. Also, bring a credit or debit card. Cash transactions on flights are a thing of the past.

- If you've never flown before, educate yourself or your autistic child about the steps of takeoff, flight, landing, what turbulence is like, etc. The sound of the wheels being tucked into the fuselage can terrify a spectrum person if they don't know the cause of it.

- Wait another year or two and buy a flying car. They're coming onto the market at only a few hundred thousand euros.

▶ **Trolls and trolling behavior** A troll is a coward, a keyboard warrior who says things to or about other people online that they wouldn't dare to say to their face. I don't really believe people are intrinsically trolls, but many of us do engage in troll-like behavior online.

Trolls are negative, confrontational, often unreasonable. They will rush to judgment, take things you said out of context and are quick to think the worst. Sometimes they will gossip and lie about a person or spread deliberate untruths. Sometimes they are just plain mean. Trolls will sometimes act like a victim of an unjust act when they are really the perpetrators. Trolls will sometimes stalk you. Often they start out as flatterers, hangers-on. Then they turn and reveal their nastiness.

One weapon of the troll is the internet group, such as those people create on Facebook. There they can get together with other trolls, or perfectly innocent, unsuspecting people, and spread their vicious nonsense.

Another, secret weapon of the troll is *political correctness*, which sprang up in the '90s as a result of centuries of bigotry and ignorance against minorities and those who are different. Unfortunately, since then it has suffered widespread abuse, most notably on the internet. A lot of trolls use political correctness to lambaste anything a person says that they might disagree with, especially if it calls their own behavior into question. Trolls have to be able to rationalize their behaviors to make them okay. Any challenge to that behavior can be seen as politically incorrect, insensitive or bullying. So a lot of bullies cry "bully" to silence those they disagree with.

It's a sad state of affairs, and when you are confronted by a troll, it's best to walk away. Once you engage in philosophical discussion with one of these club-carrying hotheads, there's never going to be a good outcome.

Not everyone you disagree with is a troll and even two fairly decent people can get into it online, especially over politics…yikes! You can engage if the person is reasonable, polite and respectful of different opinions. Resolving disputes can be very satisfying and contribute to our growth as people and as debaters, something those on the spectrum have always had a hard time doing.

Be warned that with every bit of increased fame or online presence you have, the more likely you are to attract trolls. Like crabs in a barrel, they don't want to let you go, and they don't want you to rise too high, so they'll grab you with their pincers and try to hang on as you scramble to rise above.

▶ **Trust** is something we on the spectrum may give to virtually everyone we meet. I think the idea of unprovoked hostility or cunning, or not having our best interest at heart, is something that might not occur to us in the present, even if we've encountered it many times in the past. It has slowly come to be understood by me that perhaps most non-Aspies do not do this. For them, trust is something earned; another person's nature learned, slowly, over time. We on the spectrum use our spidey-sense to glean whether we like the feel of someone.

News flash: We aren't always right. Or else, we're right but ignore our gut. We must learn to approach each person we meet not as someone to be trusted, and perhaps not as someone to be mistrusted, but as an *unknown quantity*. People must prove themselves worthy of our trust.

This is perhaps the most difficult and important lesson for us. If we trust everyone, we are certain to be disappointed and disillusioned many times in life. We are certain to find ourselves angered, having meltdowns, burning bridges, etc. The best cure is prevention: do not invest trust in those who have not proven themselves worthy to receive it.

This is difficult when you have no filter. Many of us give ourselves away. We say too much, too soon, to strangers we meet, on Facebook, on first dates. We don't have the same time schematic in our heads. I've already mentioned that many have said to me that they could love anyone who loved them back. Non-autistics and emotionally healthy Aspies will not feel this way. If you *assume* you could love someone and they you, you will come on way too trusting, like one half of an old married couple without the benefit of history or mutuality.

To keep our trust, as the parent, friend, sibling or professional associate of an Aspie, you have to be sure not to lie to us. If you do and we catch you, we may forget and forgive the first few times (or a thousand), but once that bridge of trust is damaged beyond hope, we'll just blow it up. Many of us just don't know how to keep people at arm's length, so we just cut them out of our lives forever (see *Burning bridges*). To us, lies are a virus. Conversations and relationships are difficult enough for our hard drives to process without throwing in a virus.

U

▶ **Uncertainty** (see *Surprises*, *Ritual and routine*) "Nothing is certain in life except death and taxes," said Ben Franklin. That's true for most of us. There's a slow realization, over time, that we don't know it all, that certain things might not be carved into the stone of destiny as we hoped, that we might fail at some things, or have to try much harder than we thought to succeed.

A strong spiritual or scientific belief in the circle of life will help with this in the larger sense. In the day-to-day, practical sense, tangible items such as lists of things to do help us stay organized, grounded and moving forward. GPS, phones, maps, photos, sensory toolkits, all help with the uncertainty inherent in moving into unknown situations.

Some fear of the unknown comes with reliance on parents, partners, jobs, schools and other situations which we have had to support us for some time, and the concern that we won't be able to survive without them. Time and again we see people labeled "disabled" doubting their ability to self-maintain and time and again we see it's possible with the right training and starter kit: apartment, job, etc. In fact, we may find that the unknown becomes the new known very quickly and that we love it more than what we had before.

▶ **Underestimated** This pertains to two things. One, how the impact of Asperger's and autistic traits is often underestimated by others, and two, how people on the spectrum are often underestimated (see *Misunderstood*). Too often we will hear things like "Lighten up, take it easy, relax, go with the flow, can't you just deal with it?" and so on. While it is true that we can learn to improve our sensory, social and cognitive issues through all the advice in this book, it doesn't happen overnight. And the one thing that makes a person rebel against changing is not having empathy and understanding for their current situation or crisis. You know how much your AS qualities impact you, whether positively or negatively, so if there are those who don't want to hear about it, you will probably just waste your time and effort trying to make them get it.

As with many aspects of your AS, how you say something will affect how it's received by others and how you feel about yourself afterward. "I will go to the party, but only for a short time. I like people but you know how social events wear me down" will likely go over better than saying, "My Asperger's makes parties difficult." One is much more positive, and you really can't argue with it, while the second is coming from a more negative place and opens the door to argument and contradiction.

If you and your abilities are being underestimated, welcome to the club. It happens to the best of us, on and off the spectrum. Put your nose to the grindstone, study, work, create, and prove the doubters wrong. As Frank Sinatra famously said, "The best revenge is success." He actually said "massive success," but we don't all get to the level of cultural icon, so I've culled it a bit. Of course, success doesn't always guarantee happiness, but it does add to self-esteem. Never live for the approval of others, though, just do what you do, the best you can do, and results will surely follow.

▶ **Vacations** (see *Rest and relaxation*, *Travel*)

▶ **Validation** means being legitimized in some way. Some find the validation of diagnosis a huge relief after a lifetime of struggle and being misunderstood. Others find the validation of success very satisfying after a period of hard work and uncertainty. When one has not accomplished very much in life, validation can be missing. While approval starts within, external validation is a human need; we aren't all saints. Taking steps toward success means setting achievable goals that can boost self-esteem along the way, to keep you going.

Sometimes one must be patient: our good works can take time to bear the fruit of validation, big or small.

▶ **Victim** We have all been victims and probably more than once: whether of fate, circumstance, crime, violence, deception, or of betrayal and treachery. What we do afterward determines a lot: how well we recover, how quickly, how we handle things in future, and how we view ourselves. Our usual m.o. may be to fall into despair for a time, self-pity and then lasting depression. One can refuse to be a victim, or at least to stay one.

I'm not victim-blaming, I despise the clichéd idea in some psychological circles that says no one can hurt us, because then people can act meanly and be off the hook. However, in many situations, no one party is completely innocent. In other words, we may have put ourselves in harm's way, not listened to our instincts or the wisdom of ourselves or others. The antidote to being a victim is to use it, use the accident or whatever it was. We can learn from it, and sometimes we can turn things around. The important thing, as with depression, is to take action and regain your power. As I stated in that entry, this can take a myriad of forms. Healthy forms are what I'm suggesting here, not revenge or anything destructive. Everyone will be a victim at one point. But we don't stay victims unless we allow it, choose it, wallow in it. Live for yourself, no one else can.

▶ **Video games** Many of you love to play video games. I get it, the omnipotence, the power, the escape. It's just plain fun and there's nothing wrong with that. If, however, you fall into your console and cannot bear to come out, methinks it might be time for a reboot.

One Christmas a group hacked into video game consoles. Kids around the world didn't know what to do with themselves because they couldn't use their damn thumbs for a day. On international news, they whined and moaned because they could not celebrate the birth of Jesus by virtually shooting others to death and stealing their cars. Clueless parents sat by their sides looking angry and distraught that Xmas was ruined!

"Oh good lord," I thought. "Go outside for heaven's sake! Go for a walk." Don't get me wrong, I'm not saying hacking is good. But it was a temporary hack and everyone knew they'd be able to game online in another day or two.

I personally don't like doing things with my thumbs, not sure why, never have, probably a vestige of my past life as an ape or something, but even though I can see the appeal of playing "rock star" or whatever, moderation, moderation, moderation. You are not a bad parent if you actually set times and rules for your kid. In fact, though they balk, children secretly crave and need rules and limits.

If your video playing is usurping your life you might want to step back and think about the big picture, the one that's a helluva lot bigger than a 42" flat screen.

▶ **Violence** (see *Meltdowns*) I believe it is a sign of where we are on the evolutionary scale that we seek out violence as entertainment, and seek to perpetuate it in our worlds, in our everyday lives. Perhaps it is ancient programming. Men fight over women, women over men, tribes over territory, and so on. Time and again we see the futility and results of these spontaneous or planned conflicts but there is something in humans that makes it so.

Gentle people are more likely to feel pain at watching these events, and are more likely to try and avoid them altogether. Many people on the spectrum are gentle people. Often we have been the recipients of violence, the victims.

For now it is a fact of our world. Best thing I can offer is keep fit, keep a clear head, and if you see a situation, look at the possible ramifications if you get involved. Just because your friends want to go see someone get their head kicked in on the basketball court, listen to your gut. It's probably telling you to "run away" in the famous words of Monty Python.

▶ **Virility** (see *Gender issues, Identity*)

▶ **Vitality** (see *Diet, Exercise*) Merriam Webster defines vitality as a lively or energetic quality: the power or ability of something to continue to live, be successful, etc. It didn't even occur to me to include this as an entry until a reader suggested it, because I tend to think of us on the spectrum as struggling to feel okay, maybe even good. The concept of vitality seemed, admittedly, too optimistic. Take a moment to think about how you feel, physically, every day. Do you have headaches, bowel problems, rashes or other skin issues? Are you lethargic, foggy, depressed, dizzy? Do you have toothaches, mouth ulcers, bad dreams, insomnia? Modern medicine, at least the kind that can afford national commercials, would have us think there's a pill for all those things, but as we all know, there are side effects to all medications. The goal of every person reading this is to feel as good as they possibly can, every day, and not to abuse themselves or suffer in silence until something gets to the breaking point. If you have dietary and other habits that you know make you feel unwell afterward, stop doing them. I'm not saying give up your two pints at the pub or your one ciggy a day if it makes you happy and doesn't seem to affect you adversely. But if it does, cut back until you feel good. It really is a lot more simple than we are led to believe. Wellness is your natural state. You are not nature's mistake. You deserve to be here and you deserve to feel as healthy and happy as anyone.

▶ **Wanderlust** (see *Identity, Travel*) While some people on the spectrum are too attached to the familiar and to their routines to travel, I know of many others, including myself, who have spent a great portion of their lives traveling and moving about, looking for a culture or climate where they felt they truly belonged. Because you only know you have Asperger's in relation to other people, it's very easy to "blame" our experiences on those around us. While you might be living in some ghoulish gulag of a suburb with Dudley Dursley as your nearest kin, usually it's the Aspie in us, which we'll bring with us wherever we go, that we are trying to get away from. We must learn to make peace with and love ourselves, otherwise we'll just be miserable somewhere else and maybe even stuck there.

▶ **Weird** is what tragically unimaginative people call the rest of us. When used as a compliment it means "wonderful." Famous people get to be weird and ordinary people love them for it. If you're weird in high school, it's doubtful people are going to look at you and say, "Oh, there goes a future film director, rock star, or Nobel-prize-winning scientist." They're more likely just going to want to throw lunch trays at your head. It comes with the territory, unless you are lucky enough to live and/or study in an environment that embraces diverse personality types.

It may be difficult sometimes, but stay weird. Find other weirdos to befriend. There are enough conformists already.

▶ **Working out** (see *Exercise*)

▶ **Writing** The mind is like a drawer full of memories and tidbits, facts, scraps and lint, and like any drawer it needs to be cleaned out now and then or it gets cluttered. There's nothing more cleansing and affirming than dumping your thoughts out on a clean surface to have a good look at them, rearranging them, throwing a few away and maybe even resolving to get a few new ones.

Journaling our thoughts and experiences is a wonderful self-help method. It can even lead to a career as a writer if you find you have an aptitude and love for it. I had an entire, large cardboard box of journals I threw away years ago. While I wish I had them, the practice they gave me writing no doubt helped lead to all the books I later had published.

Writing fiction is also good for us. We may not be able to escape our banal suburban existences as teens, but we can create entire universes where (our version of) good prevails, evil is punished and we are lords and masters of it all. Some of us even go on to be massively successful, with films and TV shows resulting from our brain babies.

People ask me for advice on writing fairly frequently. Writers write. That is all. While they may need to research, they don't need to talk about it, they don't procrastinate. It isn't a chore, it's almost automatic, like breathing. If you find it difficult but really want to have a go, set a simple task for yourself, for example one flash fiction story based on a particular topic, or one paragraph about your day. Over time, it will most likely get easier. If you tire of it or don't improve, it might not be for you. Creative expression can be done in a multitude of other ways.

I asked my friends on social media to finish this statement for me, and this is some of what I got. I thought they were charming.

▶ **You know you're an Aspie when…**

- You are eating honeycomb cereal, and you realize it's in the shape of cyclohexane!

- You could swear to God that kryptonite is a major element in fluorescent lights.

- You can't recognize your best friend because he's wearing a hat he never has before.

- You're in third grade and you occasionally teach your class.

- You understand your guinea pig nipped your fingertip because you'd been grating carrots and had the smell on your hands, but a cashier being offhand leaves you wondering for days if you said or did something wrong.

- Your nephew comes to visit for what you thought was a week but instead it's sixteen days. You fall over and instantly die of a brain aneurism.

- You think, "Why would anyone watch CSI when you could watch a factual documentary on forensics?!"

- You have a five-minute conversation with someone, then fifteen minutes later can't recognize who you were talking to…but you can remember everything she said.

- You can't figure out why the boys in school don't like you…and you chase them down to find out.

- You use *wingardium leviosa* as a sexual reference.

Z

▶ **Zen** In reality, Zen meditation is a highly disciplined, strict and arduous practice that involves breathing meditation, mindfulness, mudras, sutras, fasting and a number of other things that are really a lifestyle much more than a religion or a hobby. In everyday lingo, *Zen* has come to mean being pretty mellow about things, taking them as they come without getting upset, balking, melting down or being judgmental. It's a good goal to aim for.

Much of what we have learned in this book and in most books about self-advocacy is how to take control of ourselves, our lives, our habits, our outlook. But at the end of the day, life is unpredictable, others' behavior uncontrollable, and all you can really expect is the unexpected. Learning to be healthy, to feel vital, to allow yourself to be and breathe freely, is to allow everyone else to do the same too. Best of luck to you in this life.

Author Contact

Rudy Simone is the Founder and President of The International Aspergirl® Society
www.AspergirlSociety.com

Founder and operator of
www.Help4Aspergers.com

Musician, songwriter and producer
www.RudySimone.net

Notes

1. Simone, R. (2008) "Autism on the Rise—Theories on Causes and Cures." Available at www.help4aspergers.com/pb/wp_cded4122/wp_cded4122.html, accessed on March 29, 2016.

2. Gates, D. and Campbell-McBride, N. [Corganic: Real Food For Autism] (August 18, 2007) *Autism diet: Donna Gates & Dr. Campbell-McBride (1 of 6) [Video file].* Available at www.youtube.com/watch?v=nLP0Ijo2CK4, accessed on March 29, 2016.

3. Molhom, S. and Elliott, G. (2014) "Brainwaves May Help Gauge Autism Severity: Study." HealthDay Newsfeed, September 22. Available at http://consumer.healthday.com/cognitive-health-information-26/autism-news-51/brainwaves-may-help-gauge-autism-severity-study-691918.html, accessed on March 29, 2016.

4. American Psychiatric Association (APA) (2013) *Diagnostic and Statistical Manual of Mental Disorders, 5th Edition (DSM-5).* Washington, DC: American Psychiatric Association.

5. Lewis, C.S. (1953) *The Silver Chair.* London: Geoffrey Bles. p.18.

6. www.workplacebullying.org

7. O'Toole, J. (2012) *Asperkids.* London: Jessica Kingsley Publishers. p.27.

8. Center for Disease Control (2011) *Cognitive Impairment: A Call For Action Now!* Available at www.cdc.gov/aging/pdf/cognitive_impairment/cogimp_poilicy_final.pdf, accessed on March 29, 2016.

9. Wikipedia. (n.d.) "Conditions Comorbid to Autism Spectrum Disorders." Available at http://en.wikipedia.org/wiki/Conditions_comorbid_to_autism_spectrum_disorders, accessed on September 21, 2014.

10. www.help4aspergers.com/pb/wp_05797c6f/wp_05797c6f.html

11. http://wrongplanet.net

12. National Institute of Mental Health (2006) *Brain's Fear Center Shrinks in Autism's Most Severely Socially-Impaired.* Available at www.nih.gov/news/pr/dec2006/nimh-04b.htm, accessed on March 29, 2016.

13. www.youtube.com/user/Rudytutti

14. Chopra, D. (2006) *Life After Death.* London: Ebury Publishing.

15. Simone, R. (2010a) *Aspergirls.* London: Jessica Kingsley Publishers.

16. APA 2013.

17. Gates, D. and Schatz, L. (2011) *The Body Ecology Diet: Recovering Your Health and Rebuilding Your Immunity*. London: Hay House.

18. Body Ecology (n.d.) "Food Combining: The Little-Understood Secret to Optimal Health & Weight Revealed." Available at http://bodyecology.com/articles/food_combining_optimal_health_and_weight.php, accessed on March 30, 2016.

19. Gates and Schatz 2011.

20. Simone 2010a.

21. Simone, R. (2010b) *Asperger's on the Job*. Texas: Future Horizons.

22. Simone 2010b.

23. Simone, R. (2013) *Orsath*. New York: Kindle.

24. www.help4aspergers.com/pb/wp_cded4122/wp_cded4122.html, accessed on March 30, 2016.

25. Markram, K. and Markram, H. (2010) "The Intense World Theory—A unifying theory of the neurobiology of autism." Available at www.ncbi.nlm.nih.gov/pmc/articles/PMC3010743/, accessed on March 29, 2016.

26. Ornstein, C., Groeger, L., Tigas, M. and Grochowski Jones, R. (2014) *Dollars for Docs—How Industry Dollars Reach Your Doctor*. Available at https://projects.propublica.org/docdollars, accessed on March 29, 2016.

27. Child Welfare Information Gateway (2013) *Long-Term Consequences of Child Abuse and Neglect*. Available at www.childwelfare.gov/pubpdfs/long_term_consequences.pdf, accessed on March 29, 2016.

28. Simone 2010b.

29. Aha! Parenting (n.d.) "Foolproof Strategies for Getting Kids to Talk." Available at www.ahaparenting.com/parenting-tools/communication/foolproof-strategies-talk, accessed on April 15, 2015.

30. APA 2013.

31. Nichols, S. (2009) *Girls Growing Up on the Spectrum*. London: Jessica Kingsley Publishers.

32. Horiot, H. (2013) *The Emperor C'est Moi*. New York: Seven Stories Press.

33. Simone 2010a.

34. www.youtube.com/user/Rudytutti

35. Berlinger, J. (2012) "The 23 least sexist countries in the world.' *Business Insider*, October 25. Available at www.businessinsider.com/least-sexist-countries-in-world-2012-10?IR=T, accessed on March 30, 2016.

36. www.meetup.com

37. Simone 2010a.